The Complete
CHINESE
COOKBOOK

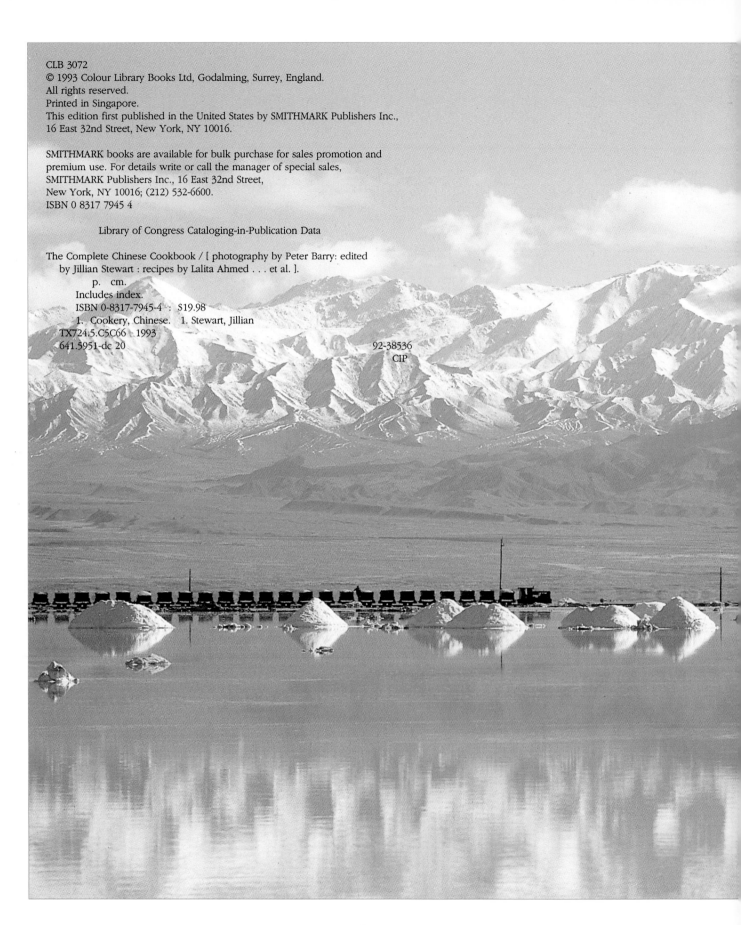

CLB 3072
© 1993 Colour Library Books Ltd, Godalming, Surrey, England.
All rights reserved.
Printed in Singapore.
This edition first published in the United States by SMITHMARK Publishers Inc.,
16 East 32nd Street, New York, NY 10016.

SMITHMARK books are available for bulk purchase for sales promotion and
premium use. For details write or call the manager of special sales,
SMITHMARK Publishers Inc., 16 East 32nd Street,
New York, NY 10016; (212) 532-6600.
ISBN 0 8317 7945 4

Library of Congress Cataloging-in-Publication Data

The Complete Chinese Cookbook / [photography by Peter Barry: edited
   by Jillian Stewart : recipes by Lalita Ahmed . . . et al.].
       p. cm.
   Includes index.
   ISBN 0-8317-7945-4 : $19.98
   1. Cookery, Chinese.   1. Stewart, Jillian
TX724.5.C5C66   1993
641.5951-dc 20
                                                    92-38536
                                                    CIP

The Complete
CHINESE
COOKBOOK

SMITHMARK

Contents

Photography by Peter Barry and Jean-Paul Paireault
Designed by Sally Strugnell
Jacket Design by Claire Leighton
Typesetting by Julie Smith
Edited by Jillian Stewart
Recipes by Lalita Ahmed, Carolyn Garner,
Moyra Frazer, Judith Ferguson and
Frederic Lebain

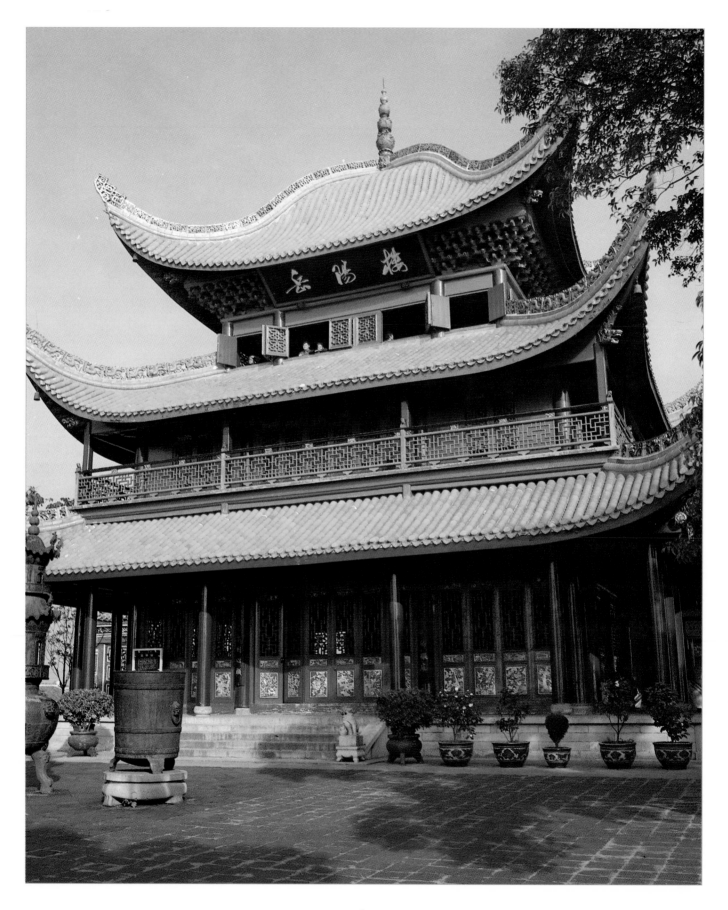

Introduction

As in any other style of cooking, Chinese food is a symbol of life and good health, forming a central part of family and social activity for many people. To the Chinese family, a meal is therefore about much more that just satisfying a physical need, it is an integral part of their social life.

In Chinese cuisine, the preparation of the food is of paramount importance. Many dishes require very fine chopping and shredding of the various ingredients, and they are combined in a very orderly manner. Those ingredients which are not available in the Western world can be substituted with similar products and alternatives to foods which may be difficult to obtain are given in the recipes. It is not necessary to use only Chinese utensils as many dishes can easily be prepared using basic kitchen equipment.

The main cooking technique used to produce Chinese food is stir-frying. A wok is ideal, but a deep non-stick pan will serve the purpose. Stir-frying requires good temperature control and this is easily learnt through practice. The wok should be heated, then the temperature reduced before adding the cooking oil. If the utensil is too hot the oil will burn, giving a charred, oily taste to the food. The heat should be progressively raised for the addition of other ingredients. The whole process may take between five and seven minutes. The most important thing to remember is to never overcook, as this will not only destroy the crispness of the food, but also its flavor and goodness.

Chinese food incorporates six basic flavors: sweet, sour, salty, spicy, pungent and hot. Their employment and respective proportions must be well balanced. Flavoring is always supplemented by ready-made sauces, the most essential of which is soy sauce.

Finally, garnishing should not be neglected, as presentation is as important as preparation. After all, what appeals to the eye also appeals to the mind and stomach! A slice of cleverly carved carrot, a thin sliver of tomato and carefully arranged Chinese parsley can add that all important dash of color.

Cooking is always a pleasure, especially Chinese cooking. It is a challenge and a way to explore one's creative talents. In any case, who does not want their efforts rewarded by the pleasure of an exquisite Chinese meal.

Soups

Peking-Style Soup
Chicken and Asparagus Soup
Turkey Soup with Black Mushrooms
Curry Soup with Meatballs
Eggflower Soup
Crab Soup with Ginger
Chicken Noodle Soup
Bamboo Shoot Soup
Chicken and Mushroom Soup
Wonton Soup
Duck Soup
Corn and Chicken Soup
Hot and Sour Soup
Crab and Watercress Soup
Noodles in Soup
Chinese Parsley and Fish Soup
Crab and Corn Soup

PEKING-STYLE SOUP

*Duck stock is the basis of this tasty, filling soup, which
contains meat and vegetables, and is delicately
flavored with sesame seeds and soy sauce.*

SERVES 4

4 slices smoked ham
1 head Chinese cabbage
3¾ cups duck stock
1 tbsp sesame seeds
Pinch chopped garlic
1 tbsp soy sauce
½ tsp white wine vinegar
Salt and pepper
1 egg yolk, beaten

1. Cut the ham into small, even-sized cubes.

2. Cut the Chinese cabbage into small pieces and simmer briskly for 10 minutes in the duck stock.

3. Stir in the sesame seeds, garlic, ham, soy sauce, vinegar and salt and pepper to taste.

4. Cook for 10 minutes over a gentle heat. Using a teaspoon, drizzle the beaten egg yolk into the soup. Serve immediately.

TIME: Preparation takes about 5 minutes and cooking takes approximately 20 minutes.

VARIATION: Replace the smoked ham with a different smoked meat.

WATCHPOINT: The smoked ham is likely to change color during cooking.

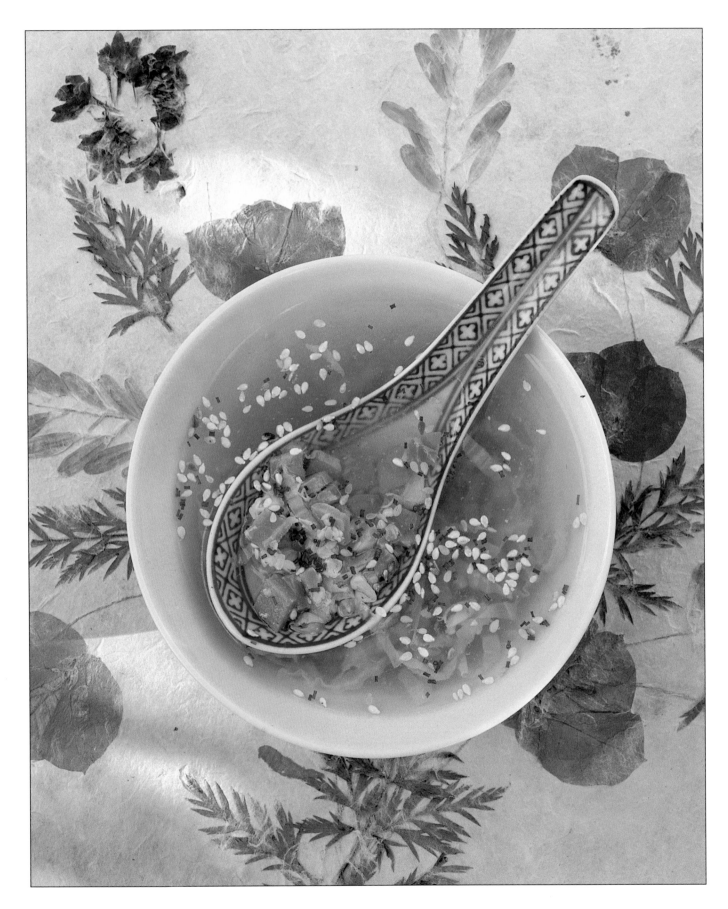

CHICKEN AND ASPARAGUS SOUP

This special occasion soup is sure to impress your guests.

SERVES 4

1lb chicken pieces
1 onion, peeled and chopped roughly
1 carrot, chopped roughly
1 stick celery, chopped roughly
4 peppercorns
5 cups water
Salt
Pepper
10oz can asparagus pieces

Garnish
Chopped parsley

1. Remove chicken meat from bones and cut into fine shreds.

2. Put chicken bones, onion, carrot, celery, peppercorns and water in wok, and season with salt and pepper. Bring to the boil, reduce heat, and simmer for 30 minutes. Strain and return stock to wok.

3. Add chicken shreds, and simmer until chicken is cooked. Add undrained asparagus pieces. Adjust seasoning. Serve sprinkled with chopped parsley.

TIME: Preparation takes 10 minutes, cooking takes 45 minutes.

COOK'S TIP: If you can afford fresh asparagus, it's taste is better than the canned variety.

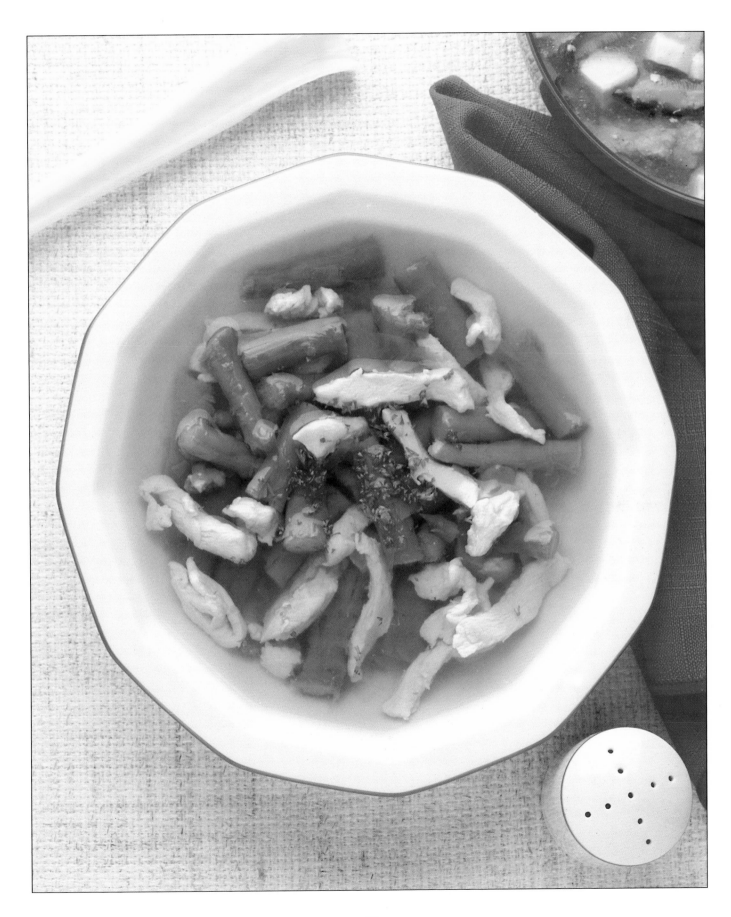

TURKEY SOUP WITH BLACK MUSHROOMS

An unusual blend of flavors which makes a tasty, warming soup.

SERVES 4

6oz turkey breast meat
1 tbsp sesame oil
2oz dried Chinese black mushrooms,
    soaked for 15 minutes in warm water
3¾ cups chicken stock
1 tbsp soy sauce
1 slice fresh root ginger
Salt and pepper

1. Cut the turkey meat into thick slices and then into small cubes.

2. Heat the sesame oil in a wok and stir-fry the meat until brown. Remove from the pan and drain off any excess oil.

3. Cook the mushrooms in boiling, salted water for 10 minutes. Rinse and drain well.

4. Place the mushrooms in a saucepan with the stock. Stir in the meat, soy sauce, ginger, and salt and pepper to taste.

5. Bring to the boil and then simmer gently for 15 minutes.

6. Remove the slices of ginger just before serving. Serve the soup very hot.

TIME: Preparation takes about 8 minutes and cooking takes approximately 35 minutes.

SERVING IDEA: Sprinkle the soup with 1 tbsp chopped fresh chives before serving.

WATCHPOINT: Don't forget to remove the slice of ginger before serving.

Curry Soup with Meatballs

A hearty soup which is perfect for heating up a cold winter night.

SERVES 4

Meatballs
8oz lean ground beef
1 clove garlic, crushed
1 onion, peeled and finely chopped
½ tsp salt
½ tsp curry powder, or ¼ tsp curry paste
½ tsp ground cinnamon
½ tsp ground cloves
½ tsp ground pepper
½ cup breadcrumbs
1 small egg, lightly beaten

Peanut oil

Broth
1 tsp garam masala
1 tsp turmeric
1 onion, peeled and finely chopped
1 tsp curry leaves
2½ cups water
1 clove garlic, crushed
½ cup shredded coconut, soaked in 1
   cup hot water for 15 minutes.

1. Mix together meatball ingredients, and form into small balls about the size of walnuts.

2. Heat wok, add oil and, when hot, fry meatballs. When browned well all over, remove with a slotted spoon, and drain on paper towels.

3. Carefully drain oil from wok. Add 1 tsp of oil, and fry spices for the broth for 30 seconds.

4. Add onion, curry leaves, and garlic, and cook together for 3 minutes.

5. Meanwhile, strain coconut in a sieve, press out as much liquid as possible, and discard the pulp.

6. Add water and coconut milk to the wok and simmer together for 5 minutes.

7. Adjust seasoning. Strain soup and return to wok. Add meatballs and simmer a further 5 minutes. Serve hot.

TIME: Preparation takes 30 minutes, cooking takes 20 minutes.

BUYING GUIDE: You will often find curry leaves in jars on the spice counter in supermarkets.

EGGFLOWER SOUP

The exotic name of this soup is derived from the appearance of the egg in the soup.

SERVES 4

14oz can plum tomatoes
1 tbsp light soy sauce
2½ cups chicken stock
2 eggs, lightly beaten
2 green onions, chopped finely

---

1. Drain and chop tomatoes, removing pips, and reserve juice.

2. Bring soy sauce, tomato juice and stock to the boil in the wok. Add tomatoes and half the green onions, and cook for 2 minutes.

3. Pour beaten eggs in gradually, stirring continuously.

4. Serve immediately, sprinkled with remaining green onions.

TIME: Preparation takes 10 minutes, cooking takes 10 minutes.

CRAB SOUP WITH GINGER

*This delicately flavored soup, with fresh crab and a
hint of ginger, is perfect for serving at a special dinner.*

SERVES 4

1 carrot, chopped
1 onion, chopped
½ leek, chopped
1 bay leaf
2 medium-sized crabs
3¾ cups fish stock
1-inch piece of fresh ginger root, chopped
1 tsp Sake Chinese wine (optional)
Salt and pepper

1. Make a vegetable stock by putting the carrot, onion, leek and bay leaf into a saucepan with a large quantity of water. Bring to the boil and add the crabs. Allow to boil briskly for 20 minutes or until cooked.

2. Remove the crabs when cooked and allow to cool. Once cooled, break off the pincers and break the joints, cut open the back and open the claws. Carefully remove all the crab meat.

3. Bring the fish stock to the boil and add the ginger, Sake and the crab meat. Boil for 15 minutes.

4. Check the seasoning, adding salt and pepper as necessary. Serve very hot.

TIME: Preparation takes about 40 minutes and cooking takes approximately 35 minutes. It takes about 30 minutes for the crab to cool, before you can comfortably remove the meat with your fingers.

WATCHPOINT: Allow plenty of time for opening the crab and removing all the meat. If time does not permit preparing fresh crab, use canned crab meat.

COOK'S TIP: Prepare the soup the day before serving. If allowed to rest overnight, the flavor of the soup will develop deliciously. Reheat gently just before serving.

CHICKEN NOODLE SOUP

A warming soup enhanced by filling noodles.

SERVES 4-6

1lb Shanghai noodles, or very thin
    noodles
2 tbsps oil
8oz cooked chicken, cubed
6oz Chinese white cabbage or ordinary
    white cabbage, shredded
6 cups chicken stock

Seasoning
½ tsp sugar
½ tsp salt
2 tsps Shao Hsing wine or dry sherry
    (optional)
½ tsp monosodium glutamate
2 tsps light soy sauce

---

1. Add the noodles to a large pan of
boiling water. Stir to loosen the bundles
and boil for 4-5 minutes. (The noodles
should be just tender but not
overcooked.) Drain noodles well.

2. Meanwhile, heat the oil in the wok and
fry the chicken for 1-2 minutes. Remove
the chicken and then fry the cabbage in
the same oil for 2 minutes.

3. Add the seasoning ingredients and stir
fry for 1 minute. Add the chicken and
cook for a further 1-2 minutes until the
cabbage is tender. Add the stock and
bring to the boil.

4. Divide noodles among 6-8 warm soup
bowls and add the hot soup. Serve
immediately.

TIME: Preparation takes 10 minutes, cooking takes 10-12 minutes.

COOK'S TIP: Monosodium glutamate just adds that little bit of
extra "bite" to the flavor of a dish.

BAMBOO SHOOT SOUP

*A very decorative soup. Beaten egg sifted into the hot
soup gives a very special effect.*

SERVES 4

3oz bamboo shoots, cut into thin
    matchsticks
4 dried Chinese black mushrooms, soaked
    for 15 minutes in warm water
3¾ cups chicken stock
1 tbsp wine vinegar
2 tbsps light soy sauce
Salt and pepper
½ tsp cornstarch, combined with a little
    water
1 egg
10 chives

1. Blanch the bamboo shoots in boiling,
salted water for 3 minutes. Rinse and set
aside to drain.

2. Cook the mushrooms in boiling, salted
water for 10 minutes. Rinse and set aside
to drain.

3. Bring the stock to the boil and add the
bamboo shoots, mushrooms, vinegar, and
soy sauce, and season with salt and
pepper to taste. Cook for 10 minutes.

4. Stir in the cornstarch and bring the soup
slowly back to the boil.

5. Reduce the heat. Beat the egg
thoroughly. Place the beaten egg in a
strainer and add to the soup by shaking
back and forth over the hot soup.

6. Add the chives to the soup and serve
piping hot.

TIME: Preparation takes about 5 minutes and cooking takes approximately 30 minutes.

WATCHPOINT: Make sure the soup is boiling hot before adding the beaten egg.

COOK'S TIP: Try to buy fresh chives for this soup, as they have a
much better flavor than dried chives.

CHICKEN AND MUSHROOM SOUP

A classic combination which works well.

SERVES 4

1 cup button mushrooms, sliced
½ cup dried brown mushrooms, soaked
   and then sliced
½ cup dried black mushrooms, soaked
   and then sliced
1 tbsp oil
6 cups chicken stock
1 cup shredded cooked chicken
3 green onions, finely chopped
¼ tsp monosodium glutamate (optional)
Salt to taste
1 tbsp light soy sauce
2 tsps Shao Hsing wine or dry sherry
   (optional)
Pinch ground white pepper
1 tsp cornstarch or arrowroot blended
   with 1 tbsp stock

1. Stir-fry the mushrooms in the oil for 2 minutes and then remove them.

2. Bring the stock to the boil in a large pan with the remaining ingredients, apart from the cornstarch and mushrooms.

3. Add the blended cornstarch and the mushrooms, and simmer for 1-2 minutes. Serve immediately.

TIME: Preparation takes 20 minutes, cooking takes 6-8 minutes.

COOK'S TIP: It is well worth hunting for the dried mushrooms as they taste wonderful. They are available in health food stores and Chinese supermarkets.

WONTON SOUP

*Probably the best-known Chinese soup, this recipe uses
pre-made wonton wrappers for ease of preparation.*

SERVES 6-8

20-24 wonton wrappers
½ cup finely ground chicken or pork
2 tbsps chopped Chinese parsley
    (cilantro)
3 green onions, finely chopped
1-inch piece fresh ginger, peeled
    and grated
1 egg, lightly beaten
6 cups chicken stock
1 tbsp dark soy sauce
Dash sesame oil
Salt and pepper
Chinese parsley or watercress for garnish

1. Place all the wonton wrappers on a
large, flat surface. Mix together the
chicken or pork, chopped parsley, green
onions and ginger. Brush the edges of the
wrappers lightly with beaten egg.

2. Place a small mound of mixture on one
half of the wrappers and fold the other
half over the top to form a triangle.

3. Press with the fingers to seal the edges
well.

4. Bring the stock to the boil in a large
saucepan. Add the filled wontons and
simmer 5-10 minutes or until they float to
the surface.

5. Add remaining ingredients to the soup,
using only the leaves of the parsley or
watercress for garnish.

TIME: Preparation takes 25-30 minutes, cooking takes about 5-10 minutes.

VARIATION: Use equal quantities of crabmeat or shrimp to fill the wontons
instead of chicken or pork.

BUYING GUIDE: Wonton wrappers are sometimes called wonton skins. They
are available in specialty shops, delicatessens and Chinese supermarkets.

DUCK SOUP

The perfect start to a Chinese meal,
and it doesn't take too long either.

SERVES 4

---

2 green onions, finely chopped
1 tbsp cooked oil
1-inch fresh root ginger, peeled and
　　finely chopped
4oz cooked duck meat, chopped
4oz winter melon, thinly sliced
6 cups chicken stock
Salt to taste
Pinch monosodium glutamate (optional)
1 tbsp Shao Hsing wine or dry sherry
　　(optional)
1 tsp arrowroot or cornstarch blended
　　with 1 tbsp stock
Freshly ground black pepper to taste

1. Fry green onions in the oil for 1 minute.

2. Add ginger and duck meat. Stir-fry for 1 minute.

3. Add winter melon and stir-fry for a further 1-2 minutes and then add stock and the remaining ingredients.

4. Gently simmer for 2-3 minutes until the soup becomes clear. Serve immediately.

TIME: Preparation takes 10 minutes, cooking takes 8 minutes.

COOK'S TIP: Use the leftovers from a recipe such as Peking Duck for the meat in this recipe.

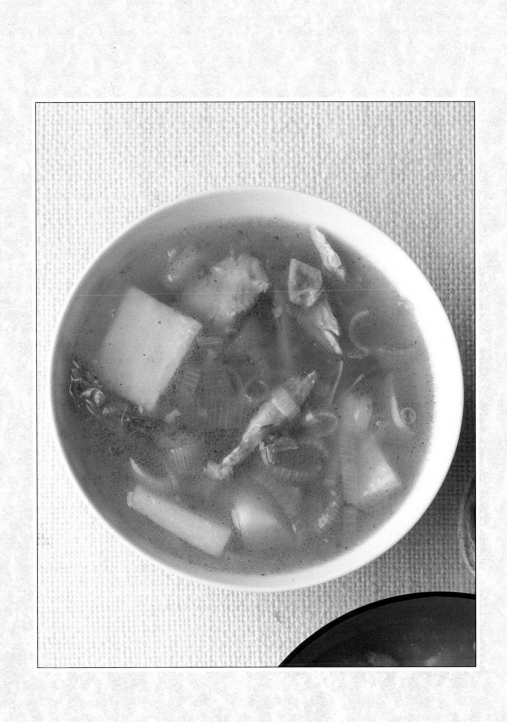

CORN AND CHICKEN SOUP

A classic soup which is still a great favorite.

SERVES 4

1 chicken, with giblets
8oz can creamy corn
1 onion, peeled and chopped roughly
1 carrot, scraped and chopped roughly
1 stick celery, chopped
6 peppercorns
Parsley stalks
1 bay leaf
1 quart water
Salt
Pepper

Garnish
Chopped parsley or chives

1. Clean chicken, and cut into quarters. Put into wok with giblets, chopped vegetables, peppercorns, bay leaf, parsley stalks, seasoning and water.

2. Bring to the boil. Reduce heat and simmer for 30 minutes. Strain and return stock to wok.

3. Discard the vegetables and giblets. Remove meat from chicken and cut into fine shreds.

4. Add undrained corn to stock, and bring to boil. Simmer for 5 minutes.

5. Add chicken and cook for 1 minute.

6. Sprinkle with chopped parsley or chives. Serve hot.

TIME: Preparation takes 15 minutes, cooking takes 45 minutes.

HOT AND SOUR SOUP

*A very warming soup, this is a favorite
in winter in Peking. Add chili sauce
and vinegar to suit your taste.*

SERVES 4-6

2oz pork
3 dried Chinese mushrooms, soaked in
    boiling water for 5 minutes and
    chopped
½ cup peeled, uncooked shrimp
6 cups chicken stock
1oz bamboo shoots, sliced
3 green onions, shredded
Salt and pepper
1 tbsp sugar
1 tsp dark soy sauce
½ tsp light soy sauce
1-2 tsps chili sauce
1½ tbsps vinegar
Dash sesame seed oil and rice wine or
    sherry
1 egg, well beaten
2 tbsps water mixed with 1 tbsp
    cornstarch

1. Trim any fat from the pork and slice it
into shreds about 2 inches long and less
than ½-inch thick.

2. Soak the mushrooms in boiling water
until softened. Place the pork in a large
pot with the shrimp and stock. Bring to
the boil and then reduce the heat to allow
to simmer gently for 4-5 minutes. Add all
the remaining ingredients except for the
egg, and cornstarch and water mixture.
Cook a further 1-2 minutes over low heat.

3. Remove the pan from the heat and add
the egg gradually, stirring gently until it
forms threads in the soup.

4. Mix a spoonful of the hot soup with the
cornstarch and water mixture and add to
the soup, stirring constantly.

5. Bring the soup back to simmering point
for 1 minute to thicken the cornstarch.
Serve immediately.

TIME: Preparation takes about 25 minutes, cooking takes 7-8 minutes.

PREPARATION: Vary the amount of chili sauce to suit your own taste.

VARIATION: Hot and Sour Soup is very versatile. Substitute other ingredients such as
chicken, crabmeat, bean sprouts, spinach or green cabbage.

WATCHPOINT: The soup must be hot enough to cook the egg when it is added, but not so
hot that the egg sets immediately.

CRAB AND WATERCRESS SOUP

Crab and watercress make a great combination in this quick soup.

SERVES 4-6

6 cups chicken stock
4oz white crab meat, shredded
2 green onions, finely chopped
2 bunches watercress, finely chopped
Salt and freshly ground black pepper to
    taste
1 tsp cornstarch or arrowroot
1 tbsp water
2 tsps light soy sauce
A few drops sesame oil

1. Bring the stock to the boil with the crab meat, onions and watercress and simmer for 4-5 minutes. Add salt and pepper to taste.

2. Mix the cornstarch with the water and add to the soup. Allow to simmer for a further 2 minutes.

3. Add soy sauce and sesame oil, mix well and simmer for 2 minutes. Serve immediately.

TIME: Preparation takes 10 minutes, cooking takes 8-9 minutes.

BUYING GUIDE: Ensure the watercress is not limp – it deteriorates rapidly once it reaches the supermarket.

NOODLES IN SOUP

A simple soup which is extremely tasty.

SERVES 4-6

1lb small rounds of noodle cakes
Salt
6 cups chicken or beef broth, or
    thick stock
4oz cooked shredded chicken
2 eggs, hard-cooked and sliced
4oz Chinese napa cabbage, finely
    shredded (or iceberg lettuce)
2 green onions, thinly sliced

1. Cook the noodles in boiling, salted water for 5 minutes. Drain thoroughly.

2. Heat the broth or stock and add salt to taste. Serve the cooked noodles in bowls, and pour over the hot broth.

3. Garnish with chicken, sliced eggs, cabbage and green onions, and serve.

TIME: Preparation takes 10 minutes, cooking takes 6-8 minutes.

BUYING GUIDE: Noodles are available in different thicknesses – buy the thinest for soups.

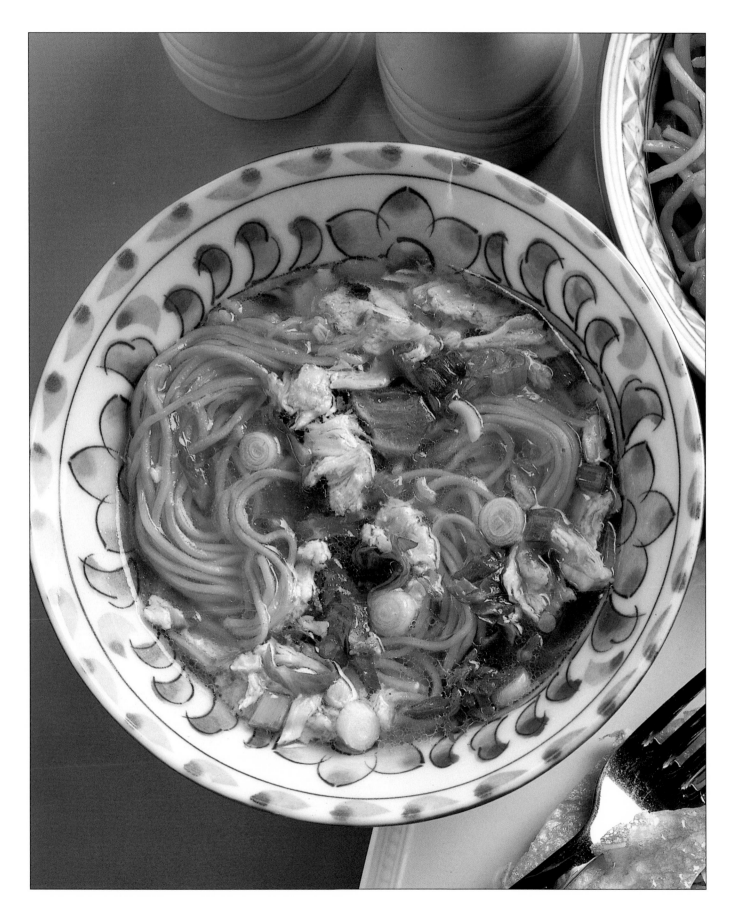

CHINESE PARSLEY AND FISH SOUP

*Chinese parsley is just another name for cilantro,
which is available in most good supermarkets.*

SERVES 4

1lb white fish fillet, cut into 6 even-
  sized pieces
4 cups chicken stock
½-inch fresh root ginger, peeled and
  thinly sliced
Salt to taste
Freshly ground black pepper to taste
Pinch monosodium glutamate (optional)
2 green onions, finely chopped
½ tsp arrowroot or cornstarch
2 sprigs Chinese parsley, finely chopped
18-20 thin cucumber slices

1. Wash fish in cold water and gently simmer in chicken stock for 2-3 minutes. Remove the fish pieces carefully.

2. Add ginger, salt, pepper, monosodium glutamate and green onion, and simmer the stock for 2-3 minutes. Strain.

3. Dissolve arrowroot in 1 tbsp water or cold stock and add to the soup. Simmer for 2 minutes until the soup thickens.

4. Add fish pieces and bring back to the boil. Serve in soup bowls, sprinkled with chopped parsley and cucumber slices.

TIME: Preparation takes 10 minutes, cooking takes 7-8 minutes.

COOK'S TIP: Use your favorite white fish for this recipe.

CRAB AND CORN SOUP

Creamed corn and succulent crabmeat
combine to make a velvety rich soup. Whisked
egg whites add an interesting texture.

SERVES 4-6

4 cups chicken or fish stock
12oz creamed corn
4oz crabmeat
Salt and pepper
1 tsp light soy sauce
2 tbsps cornstarch
3 tbsps water or stock
2 egg whites, whisked
4 green onions for garnish

1. Bring the stock to the boil in a large pan. Add the corn, crabmeat, seasoning and soy sauce. Allow to simmer for 4-5 minutes.

2. Mix the cornstarch and water or stock and add a spoonful of the hot soup. Return the mixture to the soup and bring back to the boil. Cook until the soup thickens.

3. Whisk the egg whites until soft peaks form. Stir into the hot soup just before serving.

4. Slice the onions thinly on the diagonal and scatter over the top to serve.

TIME: Preparation takes about 10 minutes, cooking takes about 8-10 minutes.

PREPARATION: Adding the egg whites is optional.

WATCHPOINT: Do not allow the corn and the crab to boil rapidly; they will both toughen.

ECONOMY: Use crab sticks instead of crabmeat.

VARIATION: Chicken may be used instead of the crabmeat and the cooking time increased to 10-12 minutes.

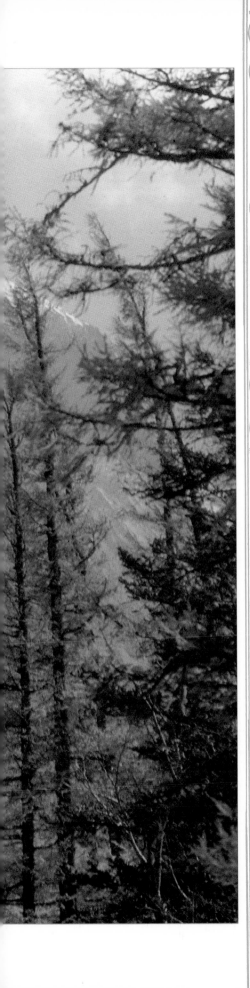

Snacks and Appetizers

Quick-Fried Shrimp
Pot Sticker Dumplings
The Peking Duck
Rice Paper Shrimp Parcels
Cantonese Egg Fu Yung
Barbecued Spare Ribs
Shrimp Fu Yung
Sesame Chicken Wings
Noodles with Ginger and Oyster Sauce
Spring Rolls
Scrambled Eggs with Shrimp
Szechuan Bang Bang Chicken
Sesame Shrimp Toasts with
Crispy Seaweed
Shanghai Noodles
Steamed Cabbage Rolls with
Fish and Crab-Meat
Snow Peas with Shrimp

QUICK-FRIED SHRIMP

*Prepared with either raw or cooked shrimp, this is
an incredibly delicious appetizer that is extremely easy to cook.*

SERVES 4-6

2lbs cooked shrimp in their shells
2 cloves garlic, crushed
1-inch piece fresh ginger, finely
    chopped
1 tbsp chopped fresh Chinese parsley
    (cilantro)
3 tbsps oil
1 tbsp rice wine or dry sherry
1½ tbsps light soy sauce
Chopped green onions to garnish

1. Shell the shrimp except for the very tail
ends. Place the shrimp in a bowl with the
remaining ingredients, except for the
garnish, and leave to marinate for 30
minutes.

2. Heat a wok and add the shrimp and
their marinade. Stir-fry briefly to heat the
shrimp.

3. Chop the onions roughly or cut into
neat rounds. Sprinkle over the shrimp to
serve.

TIME: Preparation takes about 30 minutes for the shrimp to marinate.
Cooking takes about 2 minutes.

WATCHPOINT: Do not overcook the shrimp as they will toughen.

VARIATION: If uncooked shrimp are available, stir-fry with their marinade
until they turn pink.

POT STICKER DUMPLINGS

*So called because they are fried in very little oil,
they will stick unless they are brown and crisp
on the bottom before they are steamed.*

MAKES 12

Dumplings
1½ cups all-purpose flour
½ tsp salt
3 tbsps oil
Boiling water

Filling
¾ cup finely ground pork or chicken
4 water chestnuts, finely chopped
3 green onions, finely chopped
½ tsp five spice powder
1 tbsp light soy sauce
1 tsp sugar
1 tsp sesame oil

1. Sift the flour and salt into a large bowl and make a well in the center. Pour in the oil and add enough boiling water to make a pliable dough. Add about 4 tbsps water at first and begin stirring with a wooden spoon to gradually incorporate the flour. Add more water as necessary. Knead the dough for about 5 minutes and allow to rest for 30 minutes.

2. Divide the dough into 12 pieces and roll each piece out to a circle about 6 inches in diameter.

3. Mix all the filling ingredients together and place a mound of filling on half of each circle. Fold over the top and press the edges together firmly. Roll over the joined edges using a twisting motion and press down to seal.

4. Pour about ⅛ inch of oil in a large frying pan, preferably cast iron. When the oil is hot, add the dumplings flat side down and cook until nicely browned.

5. When the underside is brown, add about 3 fl oz water to the pan and cover it tightly.

6. Continue cooking gently for about 5 minutes, or until the top surface of dumplings is steamed and appears cooked. Serve immediately.

TIME: Preparation takes about 50 minutes including the standing time for the dough.
Cooking takes about 10-20 minutes.

PREPARATION: The pan used for cooking must have a flat base. Do not use a wok.

WATCHPOINT: Make sure the dumplings are brown and crisp on the bottom before adding
the water otherwise they really will be pot stickers!

THE PEKING DUCK

A magnificent recipe much loved by all fans of Chinese cooking.

SERVES 6

1 duck, weighing 4lbs
½ medium cucumber
4 green onions

Sauce
Small can yellow bean sauce
3 tbsps sugar
2 tbsps oil

1. Clean and dry the duck. Leave in a cool place overnight.

2. Finely shred the cucumber and green onions.

3. Preheat the oven to 400°F. Place the duck on a grill rack set on top of a baking pan. Cook the duck for 1¼ hours. The duck should be very dark and crispy.

4. For the sauce, heat 2 tbsps oil in a small pan. Add the yellow bean paste and sugar. Cook together for 1-2 minutes.

5. Peel the skin off the duck and cut into 2-inch slices. Serve on a heated platter. Carve the meat off the duck into 2-inch slices, serve on a separate platter.

6. The duck skin and meat are eaten by wrapping them in pancakes which are first of all brushed with a teaspoon of duck sauce and a layer of cucumber and green onions.

TIME: Preparation takes about 15 minutes, cooking takes nearly 2 hours.

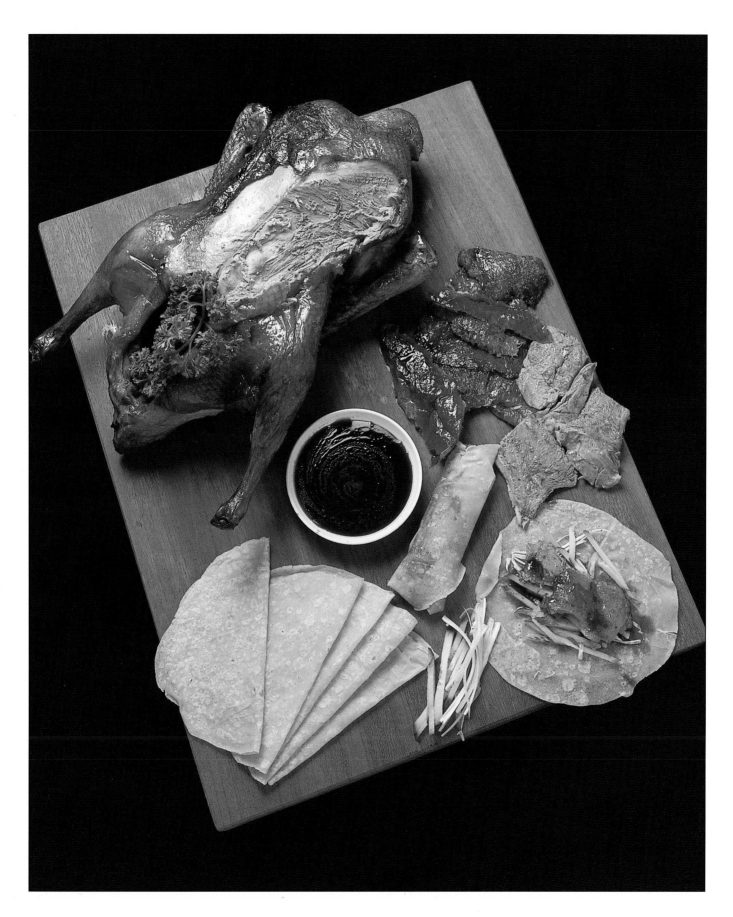

RICE PAPER SHRIMP PARCELS

The perfect nibble for a drinks party.

MAKES ABOUT 20 PARCELS

8oz shrimp, shelled and de-veined
1 egg white
½ tsp cornstarch
1 tsp Chinese wine, or 2 tsps dry sherry
1 tsp sugar
1 tsp light soy sauce
6 green onions, finely sliced
Salt
Pepper
⅔ cup peanut oil
1 packet rice paper

1. Dry the prepared shrimp on paper towels.

2. Mix egg white, cornstarch, wine, sugar, soy sauce, green onions and seasoning together. Mix in shrimp.

3. Heat peanut oil in wok until hot.

4. Wrap five or six shrimp in each piece of rice paper.

5. Gently drop in rice paper parcels and deep-fry for about 5 minutes. Serve hot.

TIME: Preparation takes 15 minutes, cooking takes 15 minutes.

CANTONESE EGG FU YUNG

As the name suggests, this dish is from Canton.
However, fu yung dishes are popular in
many other regions of China, too.

SERVES 2-3

5 eggs
½ cup shredded cooked meat, poultry
 or fish
1 stick celery, finely shredded
4 Chinese dried mushrooms, soaked in
 boiling water for 5 minutes
1 cup bean sprouts
1 small onion, thinly sliced
Pinch salt and pepper
1 tsp dry sherry
Oil for frying

Sauce
1 tbsp cornstarch dissolved in 3 tbsps
 cold water
1¼ cups chicken stock
1 tsp tomato catsup
1 tbsp soy sauce
Pinch salt and pepper
Dash sesame oil

1. Beat the eggs lightly and add the
shredded meat and celery.

2. Squeeze all the liquid from the dried
mushrooms. Remove the stems and cut
the caps into thin slices. Add the egg
mixture along with the bean sprouts and
onion. Add a pinch of salt and pepper and
the sherry and stir well.

3. Heat a wok or frying pan and pour in
about 4 tbsps oil. When hot, carefully
spoon in about 5 tbsps of the egg mixture.

4. Brown on one side, turn gently over
and brown the other side. Remove the
cooked patties to a plate and continue
until all the mixture is cooked.

5. Combine all the sauce ingredients in a
small, heavy-based pan and bring slowly
to the boil, stirring continuously until
thickened and cleared. Pour the sauce
over the Egg Fu Yung to serve.

TIME: Preparation takes 25 minutes, cooking takes about
5 minutes for the patties and 8 minutes for the sauce.

VARIATION: Use cooked shellfish such as crab or lobster,
if desired. Fresh mushrooms may be used instead of the dried ones.
Divide mixture in half or in thirds and cook one large patty per person.

ECONOMY: Left-over cooked meat such as beef, pork or chicken
can be used as an ingredient.

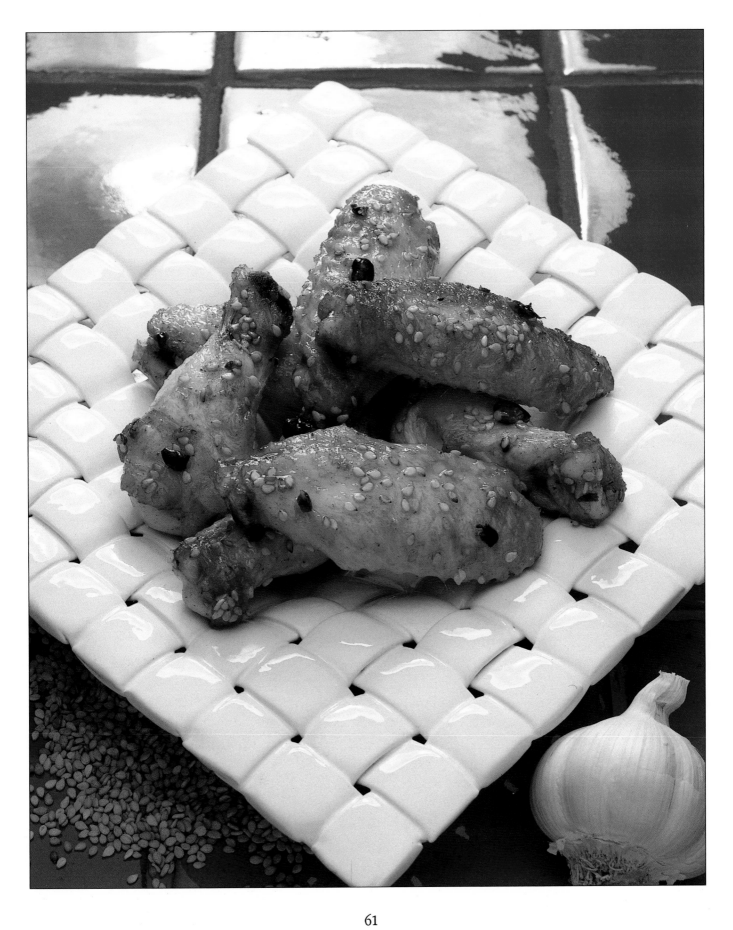

NOODLES WITH GINGER AND OYSTER SAUCE

*Noodles stir-fried with ginger, carrot and zucchini,
then served in an oyster sauce.*

SERVES 4

8oz Chinese noodles
1 carrot
1 zucchini
3 slices fresh ginger root
1 green onion, cut into thin rounds
1 tbsp oil
1 tbsp soy sauce
3 tbsps oyster sauce
Salt and pepper

1. Cook the noodles in boiling, salted water, rinse them under cold water, and set aside to drain.

2. Cut the carrot into thin strips. Thickly peel the zucchini to include a little of the flesh and cut into thin strips. Discard the center of the zucchini.

3. Peel the fresh ginger root sparingly, but remove any hard parts. Slice thinly, using a potato peeler. Cut the slices into thin strips, using a very sharp knife.

4. Heat the oil in a wok, and stir-fry the green onion for 10 seconds then add the carrot, zucchini and ginger, and stir-fry briefly.

5. Stir in the noodles and cook for 1 minute.

6. Stir in the soy and oyster sauces, and continue cooking until heated through. Season with salt and pepper and serve.

TIME: Preparation takes about 15 minutes and cooking takes approximately 15 minutes.

VARIATION: Cook the noodles in chicken stock instead of salted water
to give them extra flavor.

COOK'S TIP: Stir-fry the ginger and the other vegetables very quickly, to avoid browning them. Lower the heat if necessary.

SPRING ROLLS

One of the most popular Chinese hors d'oeuvres,
these are delicious dipped in sweet-sour sauce.

MAKES 12

Wrappers
1 cup all-purpose flour
1 egg, beaten
Cold water

Filling
8oz pork, trimmed and finely shredded
4oz shrimp, shelled and chopped
4 green onions, finely chopped
2 tbsps chopped fresh ginger
4oz Chinese leaves, shredded
2 cups bean sprouts
1 tbsp light soy sauce
Dash sesame seed oil
1 egg, beaten

1. To prepare the wrappers, sift the flour into a bowl and make a well in the center. Add the beaten egg and about 1 tbsp cold water. Begin beating with a wooden spoon, gradually drawing in the flour from the outside to make a smooth dough. Add more water if necessary.

2. Knead the dough until it is elastic and pliable. Place in a covered bowl and chill for about 4 hours or overnight.

3. When ready to roll out, allow the dough to come back to room temperature. Flour a large work surface well and roll the dough out to about ¼-inch thick.

4. Cut the dough into 12 equal squares and then roll each piece into a larger square about 6 x 6 inches. The dough should be very thin. Cover while preparing the filling.

5. Cook the pork in a little of the frying oil for about 2-3 minutes. Add the remaining filling ingredients, except the beaten egg, cook for 2-3 minutes and allow to cool.

6. Lay out the wrappers on a clean work surface with the point of each wrapper facing you. Brush the edges lightly with the beaten egg.

7. Divide the filling among all twelve wrappers, placing it just above the front point. Fold over the sides like an envelope.

8. Fold over the point until the filling is completely covered. Roll up as for a jelly roll. Press all the edges to seal well.

9. Heat the oil in a deep fat fryer or in a deep pan to 375°F. Depending upon the size of the fryer, place in 2-4 spring rolls and fry until golden brown on both sides. The rolls will float to the surface when one side has browned and should then be turned over. Drain thoroughly on paper towels and serve hot.

TIME: Preparation takes about 50 minutes for the wrapper dough, the filling and for rolling up. Dough must be allowed to rest for at least 4 hours before use. Cooking takes about 20 minutes.

SCRAMBLED EGGS WITH SHRIMP

Fish-flavored scrambled eggs, cooked with shrimp.

SERVES 4

12 shrimp, peeled
8 eggs, beaten
½ stick celery, cut into small dice
1 green onion, chopped
1 tsp fish sauce
Salt and pepper

1. Cut the shrimp into small pieces.

2. Stir the shrimp into the eggs and add the celery, green onion and fish sauce.

3. Season with a little salt and pepper.

4. Cook by stirring over a gentle heat. When cooked to your liking, serve immediately.

TIME: Preparation takes about 10 minutes and cooking takes approximately 10 minutes.

WATCHPOINT: The fish sauce is very salty. Only add more salt after cooking, if necessary.

Szechuan Bang Bang Chicken

This is a good dish to serve as an appetizer.

SERVES 2

2 chicken breasts
1 medium cucumber

Sauce
5 tbsps peanut butter
2 tsps sesame oil
½ tsp sugar
¼ tsp salt
2 tsps stock
½ tsp chili sauce

1. Simmer the chicken in a pan of water for 30 minutes. Remove the chicken breasts and cut them into ½-inch thick strips.

2. Thinly slice the cucumber. Spread cucumber on a large serving platter. Pile the shredded chicken on top.

3. Mix the peanut butter with the sesame oil, sugar, salt and stock. Pour the sauce evenly over the chicken.

4. Sprinkle the chili sauce evenly over the top.

Time: Cooking takes about 30 minutes, final preparation takes 5 minutes.

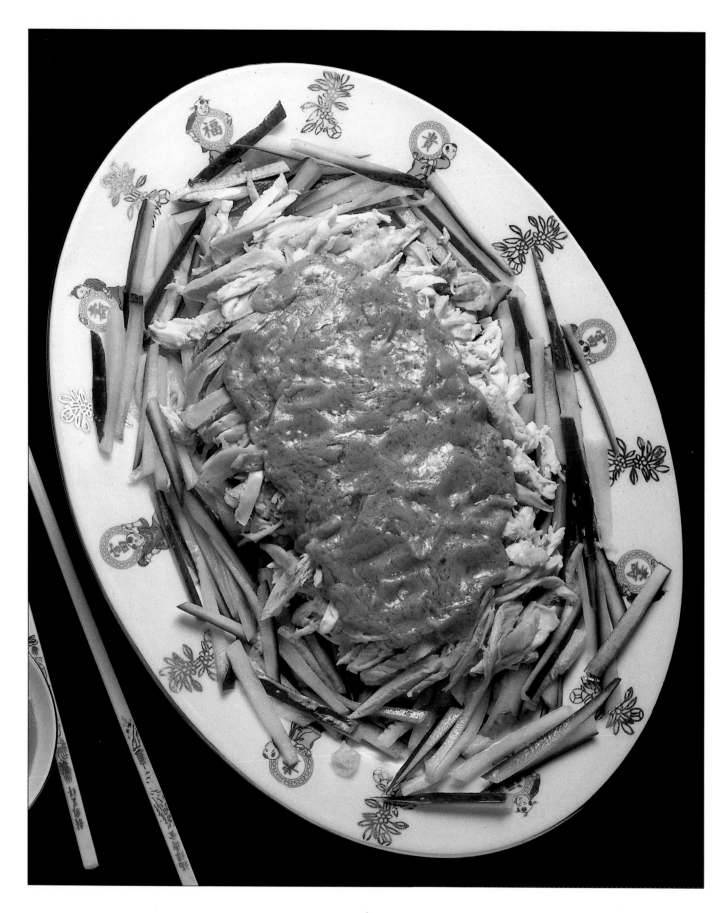

SESAME SHRIMP TOASTS WITH CRISPY SEAWEED

Have great fun trying to eat crispy seaweed with your chopsticks!

SERVES 2-4

4oz pork fat
6oz cooked shrimp
1 egg white
Salt and pepper to taste
1 tbsp cornstarch
2 slices white bread
7 tbsps sesame seeds
Oil for deep frying

Crispy Seaweed
2lbs greens
4 tbsps split almonds
Oil for deep frying
½ tsp salt
1½ tsps sugar

1. Finely chop pork fat and shrimp. Blend together well with egg white, salt, pepper and cornstarch. Spread the "paste" thickly on the 2 slices of bread. Remove the crusts.

2. Sprinkle the paste thickly with sesame seeds pressing them on well.

3. Heat the oil. Lower one slice of bread at a time into the hot oil, spread side down, for 2 minutes. Turn over and fry the other side for ½ minute. Repeat for other slice of bread.

4. Cut each shrimp toast in half, then into finger-sized strips.

5. With a very sharp knife, cut the greens into the finest shreds possible. Dry, by spreading them out on paper towels for half an hour. Deep fry, or shallow fry the almonds until golden. Drain well.

6. Heat the oil until it is about to smoke. Remove from the heat for ½ minute.

7. Add all the shreds of greens. Stir and return pan to the heat and fry for 2-3 minutes. Remove and drain well.

8. Serve the shrimp toasts and crispy seaweed on a well heated platter, sprinkle crispy seaweed evenly with salt, sugar, and almonds.

TIME: Preparation takes 10 minutes for the shrimp toasts and 5 minutes for the seaweed, cooking takes about 10 minutes for the shrimp toasts and about 3 minutes for the crispy seaweed.

BUYING GUIDE: Sesame seeds can be bought from health food stores as well as some good supermarkets.

Fish and Seafood

Singapore Fish
Cantonese Shrimp
Szechuan Fish
Shrimp and Ginger
Shrimp in Hot Sauce
Sweet-Sour Fish
Honey Sesame Shrimp
Steamed Shrimp
Whiting Fritters with Cold Fish Sauce
Shrimp with Broccoli
Szechuan Fish Steak
Crispy Fish with Chili
Seafood Chow Mein
Kung Pao Shrimp with Cashew Nuts

SINGAPORE FISH

*The cuisine of Singapore was much influenced by that of
China. In turn, the Chinese introduced ingredients
like curry powder into their cuisine.*

SERVES 4

1lb white fish fillets
1 egg white
1 tbsp cornstarch
2 tsps white wine
Salt and pepper
Oil for frying
1 large onion, cut into ½-inch
  thick wedges
1 tbsp mild curry powder
1 small can pineapple pieces, drained and
  juice reserved, or ½ fresh pineapple,
  peeled and cubed
1 small can mandarin orange segments,
  drained and juice reserved
1 small can sliced water chestnuts, drained
1 tbsp cornstarch mixed with juice of 1
  lime
2 tsps sugar (optional)
Pinch salt and pepper

1. Starting at the tail end of the fillets, skin them using a sharp knife.

2. Slide the knife back and forth along the length of each fillet, pushing the fish flesh along as you go.

3. Cut the fish into even-sized pieces, about 2 inches square.

4. Mix together the egg white, cornstarch, wine, salt and pepper. Place the fish in the mixture and leave to stand while heating the oil.

5. When the oil is hot, fry a few pieces of fish at a time until light golden brown and crisp. Remove the fish to paper towels to drain, and continue until all the fish is cooked.

6. Remove all but 1 tbsp of the oil from the wok and add the onion. Stir-fry the onion for 1-2 minutes and add the curry powder. Cook the onion and curry powder for a further 1-2 minutes. Add the juice from the pineapple and mandarin oranges and bring to the boil.

7 Combine the cornstarch and lime juice and add a spoonful of the boiling fruit juice. Return the mixture to the wok and cook until thickened, about 2 minutes. Taste and add sugar if desired.

8. Add the fruit, water chestnuts and fried fish to the wok and stir to coat. Heat through 1 minute and serve immediately.

TIME: Preparation takes about 25 minutes, cooking takes about 10 minutes.

VARIATION: Chicken may be used in place of the fish and cooked in the same way. Garnish with Chinese parsley leaves if desired.

SERVING IDEA: Serve with plain rice, fried rice or cooked Chinese noodles.

81

CANTONESE SHRIMP

*This quick and easy recipe is suitable for those
times when unexpected friends drop in for lunch.*

SERVES 2-3

3 tbsps oil
2 cloves garlic, finely crushed
1lb peeled shrimp
2 inch piece root ginger, peeled and finely
    chopped
4oz uncooked pork or bacon, finely
    chopped

Sauce
1 tbsp rice wine or dry sherry
1 tbsp light soy sauce
1 tsp sugar
1¼ cups stock or water
1 tbsp cornstarch mixed with
    2 tbsps stock or water

2-3 green onions, chopped
2 eggs, lightly beaten

1. Heat 1 tbsp oil in a wok. Add the garlic
and fry for 1 minute.

2. Add the shrimp and stir-fry for 4-5
minutes. Remove to a dish. Keep warm.

3. Add the remaining oil to the wok and
fry the ginger and pork for 3-4 minutes
until it loses its color.

4. Add the mixed sauce ingredients to the
wok and cook for 1 minute.

5. Add the onions and cook for 1 minute.
Add the beaten eggs and cook for 1-2
minutes, without stirring, until it sets.
Spoon the egg mixture over the shrimp.

6. Alternatively, add the shrimp along with
the beaten eggs. Allow the eggs to set and
then mix gently. Serve at once.

TIME: Preparation takes 10 minutes, cooking takes 15 minutes.

COOK'S TIP: Dry sherry is always a good substitute for Chinese wine so keep a bottle
specially for this purpose.

SZECHUAN FISH

The piquant spiciness of Szechuan pepper is quite different from that of black or white pepper. Beware, though, too much can numb the mouth temporarily!

SERVES 6

6 red or green chili peppers
1lb white fish fillets
Pinch salt and pepper
1 egg
6 tbsps flour
7 tbsps white wine
Oil for frying
2oz cooked ham, cut in small dice
1-inch piece fresh ginger, finely diced
½-1 red or green chili pepper, cored, seeded and finely diced
6 water chestnuts, finely diced
4 green onions, finely chopped
3 tbsps light soy sauce
1 tsp cider vinegar or rice wine vinegar
½ tsp ground Szechuan pepper (optional)
1¾ cups light stock
1 tbsp cornstarch dissolved with 2 tbsps water
2 tsps sugar

1. To prepare the garnish, choose unblemished chili peppers with the stems on. Using a small, sharp knife, cut peppers in strips, starting from the pointed end.

2. Cut down to within ½ inch of the stem end. Rinse out the seeds under cold running water and place the peppers in iced water.

3. Leave the peppers to soak for at least 4 hours or overnight until they open up like a flower.

4. Cut the fish fillets into 2-inch pieces and season with salt and pepper. Beat the egg well and add flour and wine to make a batter. Dredge the fish lightly with flour and then dip into the batter. Coat the fish well.

5. Heat a wok and when hot, add enough oil to deep-fry the fish. When the oil is hot, fry a few pieces of fish at a time, until golden brown. Drain and proceed until all the fish is cooked.

6. Remove all but 1 tbsp of oil from the wok and add the ham, ginger, diced chili pepper, water chestnuts and green onions. Cook for about 1 minute and add the soy sauce and vinegar. If using Szechuan pepper, add at this point. Stir well and cook for a further 1 minute. Remove the vegetables from the pan and set them aside.

7. Add the stock to the wok and bring to the boil. When boiling, add 1 spoonful of the hot stock to the cornstarch mixture. Add the mixture back to the stock and re-boil, stirring constantly until thickened.

8. Stir in the sugar and return the fish and vegetables to the sauce. Heat through for 30 seconds and serve at once.

TIME: Preparation takes about 30 minutes. Chili pepper garnish takes at least 4 hours to soak. Cooking takes about 10 minutes.

SHRIMP AND GINGER

An age-old combination which has stood the test of time.

SERVES 4

2 tbsps oil
1½lbs peeled shrimp
1 inch fresh root ginger, peeled and
    finely chopped
2 cloves garlic, peeled and finely chopped
2-3 green onions, chopped lengthways
    into 1-inch pieces
1 leek, white part only, cut into strips
¾ cup shelled peas
3 cups bean sprouts

Seasoning
2 tbsps dark soy sauce
1 tsp sugar
Pinch monosodium glutamate (optional)
Pinch of salt

1. Heat the oil in a wok and stir-fry the shrimp for 2-3 minutes. Remove the shrimp to a dish.

2. Reheat the oil and add the ginger and garlic, and fry for 1 minute.

3. Add the onions and stir-fry for 1 minute.

4. Add the leek, peas and bean sprouts. Fry for 2-3 minutes.

5. Sprinkle over the seasoning ingredients and return the shrimp to the wok. Cover and cook for 20 minutes. Serve immediately.

TIME: Preparation takes 10 minutes, cooking takes 10 minutes.

BUYING GUIDE: Always buy bean sprouts on the day your intend to use them, as they deteriorate rapidly.

SHRIMP IN HOT SAUCE

A quick dish that is perfect for a mid-week treat.

SERVES 2

12oz cooked unshelled shrimp

Seasoning
1 tsp malt vinegar
1 tsp Shao Hsing wine or dry sherry
Pinch salt

Sauce
1 tsp cornstarch mixed with 1 tbsp
   water
2 tsps tomato paste
Salt and freshly ground black pepper to
   taste
2 tsps sugar
½ tsp monosodium glutamate (optional)
1 tsp hot chili sauce
1 cup chicken stock

2 tbsps cooked oil
1 onion, chopped
1 stick celery, sliced
1 clove garlic, peeled and crushed

1. Wash shrimp and drain well. Mix the seasoning ingredients together.

2. Mix the sauce ingredients together in a separate bowl.

3. Heat the oil in a wok and deep-fry the shrimp for 1 minute. Remove the shrimp and drain. Keep the oil.

4. Reheat the wok and add 2 tsps oil and stir-fry the onion, celery and garlic for 1 minute.

5. Add shrimp and blended sauce ingredients. Bring to the boil and simmer gently for 3-4 minutes. Stir in the seasoning mixture.

TIME: Preparation takes 10 minutes, cooking takes 6 minutes.

SWEET-SOUR FISH

In China this dish is almost always prepared with freshwater fish, but sea bass is also an excellent choice.

SERVES 2

1 sea bass, gray mullet or carp, weighing about 2lbs, cleaned
1 tbsp dry sherry
Few slices fresh ginger
½ cup sugar
7 tbsps cider vinegar
1 tbsp soy sauce
2 tbsps cornstarch
1 clove garlic, crushed
2 green onions, shredded
1 small carrot, peeled and finely shredded
½ cup bamboo shoots, shredded

1. Rinse the fish well inside and out. Make three diagonal cuts on each side of the fish with a sharp knife.

2. Trim off the fins, leaving the dorsal fin on top.

3. Trim the tail to two neat points.

4. Bring enough water to cover the fish to boil in a wok. Gently lower the fish into the boiling water and add the sherry and ginger. Cover the wok tightly and remove at once from the heat. Allow to stand 15-20 minutes to let the fish cook in the residual heat.

5. To test if the fish is cooked, pull the dorsal fin – if it comes off easily the fish is done. If not, return the wok to the heat and bring to the boil. Remove from the heat and leave the fish to stand a further 5 minutes. Transfer the fish to a heated serving dish and keep it warm.

6. Take all but 4 tbsps of the fish cooking liquid from the wok. Add the remaining ingredients including the vegetables and cook, stirring constantly, until the sauce thickens. Spoon some of the sauce over the fish to serve and serve the rest separately.

TIME: Preparation takes about 25 minutes, cooking takes about 15-25 minutes.

COOK'S TIP: The diagonal cuts in the side of the fish ensure even cooking.

VARIATION: If desired, use smaller fish such as trout or red mullet and shorten the cooking time to 10-15 minutes.

PREPARATION: The fish may also be cooked in the oven in a large roasting pan or in greased foil sprinkled with sherry. Cook at 375°F for 10 minutes per ½-inch thickness, measured around the middle of the fish.

HONEY SESAME SHRIMP

*Shrimp sweetened with honey and sprinkled
with sesame seeds – the perfect dish to spoil yourself with.*

SERVES 4

1 cup all-purpose flour
Pinch of salt
Pepper
1 egg, lightly beaten
⅔ cup water
1lb shrimp shelled and de-veined
2 tbsps cornstarch
Oil for deep frying
1 tbsp sesame oil
2 tbsps honey
1 tbsp sesame seeds

1. Sift flour and salt and pepper into a bowl. Make a well in the center, add egg and water, and gradually mix in the flour.

2. Beat to a smooth batter and set aside for 10 minutes.

3. Meanwhile, toss shrimp in cornstarch and coat well. Shake off any excess cornstarch. Add shrimp to batter and coat well.

4. Heat oil in wok and add shrimp, a few at a time. Cook until batter is golden. Remove shrimp, drain on paper towels, and keep warm. Repeat until all shrimp have been fried.

5. Carefully remove hot oil from wok. Gently heat sesame oil in pan.

6. Add honey and stir until mixed well and heat through. Add shrimp to mixture and toss well.

7. Sprinkle over sesame seeds and again toss well. Serve immediately.

TIME: Preparation takes 20 minutes, cooking takes 20 minutes.

STEAMED SHRIMP

*Fresh shrimp, garnished with zucchini peel, steamed
and served with a fish-flavored sauce.*

SERVES 4

1 tbsp fish sauce
1 tbsp water
1 tbsp wine vinegar
1 tbsp soy sauce
2 tsps sugar
10 fresh mint leaves, finely chopped
1 shallot, chopped
Salt and pepper
12 fresh shrimp, peeled and cleaned
2 medium-sized zucchini, peeled and
   the peel cut into long strips

1. Mix together the fish sauce, water,
vinegar, soy sauce, sugar, mint, shallot
and salt and pepper. Stir well and set
aside for a least 1 hour.

2. Just before serving time, season the
shrimp with plenty of salt and pepper.

3. Roll the strips of zucchini peel around
the shrimp and cook them in a Chinese
steamer for 5 minutes.

4. Serve the shrimp piping hot,
accompanied with the sauce.

TIME: Preparation takes about 20 minutes and cooking takes about
10 minutes for 2 batches.

COOK'S TIP: If the strips of zucchini peel are not very pliable, blanch them in boiling
water for 3 seconds, before wrapping around the shrimp.

WATCHPOINT: The sauce can be prepared just before cooking the shrimp,
but it is much tastier if prepared at least 1 hour in advance.

SZECHUAN FISH STEAK

Szechuan food is hot and this recipe makes a wonderfully zippy fish dish.

SERVES 4

1½lbs haddock
2 tsps salt
2 tbsps cornstarch
1 egg

Sauce
1 large onion
2 cloves garlic
3 slices ginger root
2 chili peppers
2 slices Szechuan Ja Chai pickle (see
  Cook's Tip)
1 dried chili
Oil for deep frying
7 tbsps chicken stock
3 tbsps soy sauce
2 tbsps tomato paste
2 tbsps Hoisin sauce
1 tbsp sugar
1 tbsp wine vinegar
2 tbsps pale sherry

1. Cut fish into 2 x 1-inch oblong pieces. Rub with salt. Blend the cornstarch with the egg. Dip the fish in the egg mixture to coat on both sides.

2. Thinly slice the onion. Finely chop the garlic, ginger, chilies, pickle and dried chili.

3. Heat 4 tbsps oil in a large frying pan. Add the onion and other chopped vegetables and stir-fry for 2 minutes.

4. Add the stock, soy sauce, paste, Hoisin sauce, sugar, vinegar, and sherry. Stir over a high heat until well reduced.

5. Heat about 4 cups oil in a deep fryer. When hot, add the fish and fry for 2 minutes. Remove and drain.

6. Place them in the pan of sauce. Simmer in the sauce for 5 minutes before serving.

TIME: Preparation takes 10 minutes, cooking takes 10 minutes.

COOK'S TIP: If you cannot obtain the Ja Chai pickle, substitute your favorite hot pickle.

CRISPY FISH WITH CHILI

Choose your favorite white fish for this recipe.

SERVES 4

450g/1lb fish fillets, skinned, bones removed, and cut into 1-inch cubes

Batter
½ cup all-purpose flour
1 egg, separated
1 tbsp oil
6 tbsps milk
Salt
Oil for deep frying

Sauce
1 tsp grated root ginger
¼ tsp chili powder
2 tbsps tomato paste
2 tbsps tomato chutney
2 tbsps dark soy sauce
2 tbsps Chinese wine or dry sherry
2 tbsps water
1 tsp sugar

1 red chili, seeds removed, and sliced finely
1 clove garlic, crushed
Salt
Pepper

1. Sift the flour with a pinch of salt. Make a well in the center, and drop in the egg yolk and oil.

2. Mix to a smooth batter with the milk, gradually incorporating the flour. Beat well. Cover and set aside in a cool place for 30 minutes.

3. Whisk egg white until stiff, and fold into batter just before using.

4. Heat oil in wok. Dip fish pieces into batter and coat completely. When oil is hot, carefully lower fish pieces in until cooked through and golden brown – about 10 minutes. Remove with a slotted spoon.

5. Reheat oil and refry each fish piece for 2 minutes. Remove with a slotted spoon and drain on paper towels.

6. Carefully remove all but 1 tbsp of oil from the wok.

7. Heat oil, add chili, ginger, garlic, chili powder, tomato paste, tomato chutney, soy sauce, sugar, wine and water, and salt and pepper to taste.

8. Stir well over heat for 3 minutes. Increase heat and toss in fish pieces. Coat with sauce and, when heated through, serve immediately.

TIME: Preparation takes 40 minutes, cooking takes 30 minutes.

COOK'S TIP: Choose your favorite type of fish for this recipe.

SEAFOOD CHOW MEIN

*Chinese noodles cooked with mussels, cockles and
vegetables and served in a rich ginger
and wine flavored sauce.*

SERVES 4

8oz Chinese noodles
½ green pepper, seeded
½ red pepper, seeded
1 tbsp oil
½ tsp chopped garlic
½ tsp chopped fresh ginger root
½ green onion, chopped
5oz uncooked mussels (shelled)
2oz uncooked clams (shelled)
1 tbsp Chinese wine
2 tbsps soy sauce
Salt and pepper

1. Cook the noodles in boiling, salted water. Rinse them under cold water and set aside to drain.

2. Cut the peppers into thin slices.

3. Heat the oil in a wok and stir-fry the garlic, ginger, peppers and green onion for 1 minute.

4. Stir in the mussels, clams, Chinese wine, soy sauce and the cooked noodles.

5. Mix together well, using chopsticks. Season with salt and pepper and serve when cooked through completely.

TIME: Preparation takes about 15 minutes and cooking takes approximately 15 minutes.

VARIATION: Add other types of seafood to this dish.

WATCHPOINT: In Step 5 heat the noodles thoroughly, turning them in the sauce, to coat evenly.

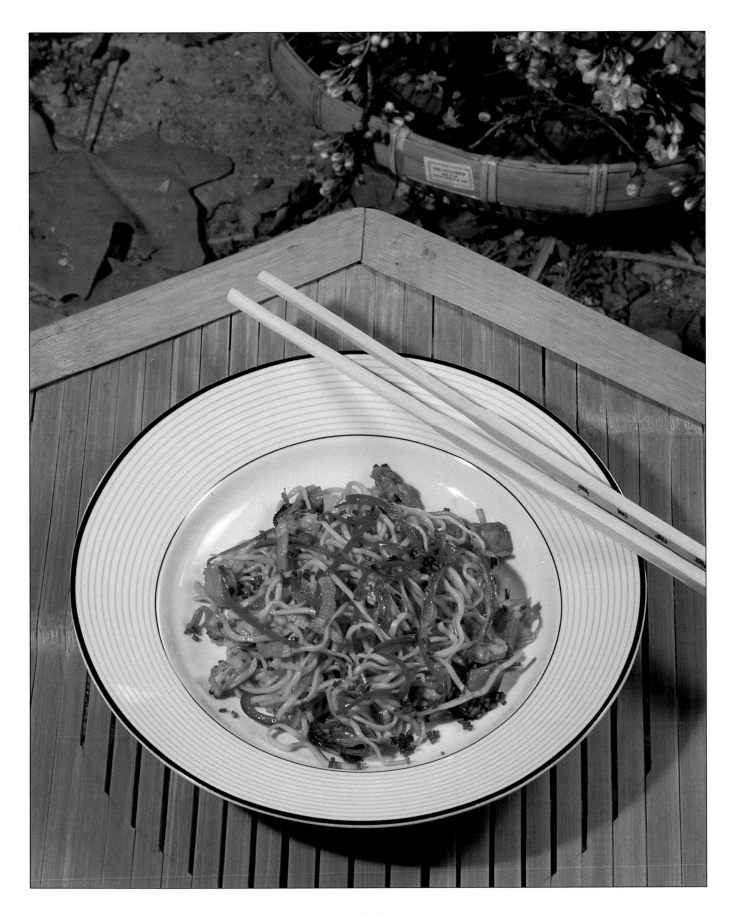

Kung Pao Shrimp with Cashew Nuts

*It is said that Kung Pao invented this dish, but
to this day no one knows who he was!*

SERVES 6

½ tsp chopped fresh ginger
1 tsp chopped garlic
1½ tbsps cornstarch
¼ tsp baking soda
Salt and pepper
¼ tsp sugar
1lb uncooked shrimp
4 tbsps oil
1 small onion, cut into dice
1 large or 2 small zucchini, cut into
   ½-inch cubes
1 small red pepper, cut into ½-inch cubes
2oz cashew nuts

Sauce
1 cup chicken stock
1 tbsp cornstarch
2 tsps chili sauce
2 tsps bean paste (optional)
2 tsps sesame oil
1 tbsp dry sherry or rice wine

1. Mix together the ginger, garlic,
1½ tbsps cornstarch, baking soda, salt,
pepper and sugar.

2. If the shrimp are unpeeled, remove the peels and the dark vein running along the rounded side. If large, cut in half. Place in the dry ingredients and leave to stand for 20 minutes.

3. Heat the oil in a wok and when hot add the shrimp. Cook, stirring over high heat for about 20 seconds, or just until the shrimp change color. Transfer to a plate.

4. Add the onion to the same oil in the wok and cook for about 1 minute. Add the zucchini and red pepper and cook about 30 seconds.

5. Mix the sauce ingredients together and add to the wok. Cook, stirring constantly, until the sauce is slightly thickened. Add the shrimp and the cashew nuts and heat through completely.

TIME: Preparation takes about 20 minutes, cooking takes about 3 minutes.

VARIATION: If using cooked shrimp, add with the vegetables.
Vary amount of chili sauce to suit your taste.

SERVING IDEA: Serve with plain or fried rice.

Meat

Pork and Shrimp Chow Mein

Lamb with Tomatoes

Sweet and Sour Beef

Pork Spare Ribs

Beef with Broccoli

Fillet Steak Chinese Style

Pork with Green Peppers

Five-Spice Beef with Broccoli

Beef with Onions

Sweet and Sour Pork

Spiced Beef

Meat and Shrimp Chow Mein

Sweet and Sour Pork and Pineapple

Stir-fry Beef with Mango Slices

Lamb Meatballs with Yogurt

Caramelized Spareribs

Beef with Green Pepper and Chilli

Beef Steak with Ginger

Pork Meat Balls in Sauce

Peking Beef

Lamb Curry

Sweet Pork with Vegetables

Braised Hong Kong Beef

Beef with Green Beans

Diced Pork with Walnuts

Beef with Tomato and Pepper in Black
Bean Sauce

Steamed Lamb with Mushroom Sauce

Pork with Black Bean Sauce

PORK & SHRIMP CHOW MEIN

Chinese chow mein dishes are usually based on noodles,
using more expensive ingredients in small amounts.
This makes economical everyday fare.

SERVES 4-6

8oz medium dried Chinese noodles
Oil
8oz pork tenderloin, thinly sliced
1 carrot, peeled and shredded
1 small red pepper, cored, seeded and
    thinly sliced
2 cups bean sprouts
2oz snow peas
1 tbsp rice wine or dry sherry
2 tbsps soy sauce
1 cup peeled, cooked shrimp

1. Cook the noodles in plenty of boiling salted water for about 4-5 minutes. Rinse under hot water and drain thoroughly.

2. Heat the wok and add oil. Stir-fry the pork 4-5 minutes or until almost cooked. Add the carrots to the wok and cook for 1-2 minutes.

3. Add the red pepper and add the remaining vegetables, wine and soy sauce. Cook for about 2 minutes.

4. Add the cooked, drained noodles and shrimp and toss over heat for 1-2 minutes. Serve immediately.

TIME: Preparation takes about 20 minutes. The noodles take 4-5 minutes to cook and the stir-fried ingredients need to cook for about 5-6 minutes for the pork and about 3 minutes for the vegetables.

VARIATION: Use green pepper instead of red, or add other vegetables such as baby corn ears, mushrooms or peas.

BUYING GUIDE: Dried Chinese noodles are available in three thicknesses. Thin noodles are usually reserved for soup, while medium and thick noodles are used for fried dishes.

SWEET AND SOUR PORK

This really needs no introduction because of its popularity.
The dish originated in Canton, but is reproduced
in most of the world's Chinese restaurants.

SERVES 2-4

1 cup all-purpose flour
4 tbsps cornstarch
1½ tsps baking powder
Pinch salt
1 tbsp oil
Water
8oz pork fillet, cut into ½-inch cubes

1 onion, sliced
1 green pepper, seeded, cored and sliced
1 small can pineapple chunks, juice
   reserved
Oil for frying

Sweet and Sour Sauce
2 tbsps cornstarch
½ cup light brown sugar
Pinch salt
½ cup cider vinegar or rice
   vinegar
1 clove garlic, crushed
1 tsp fresh ginger, grated
6 tbsps tomato catsup
6 tbsps reserved pineapple juice

1. To prepare the batter, sift the flour, cornstarch, baking powder and salt into a bowl. Make a well in the center and add the oil and enough water to make a thick, smooth batter. Using a wooden spoon, stir the ingredients in the well, gradually incorporating flour from the outside, and beat until smooth.

2. Heat enough oil in a wok to deep-fry the pork. Dip the pork cubes one at a time into the batter and drop into the hot oil. Fry 4-5 pieces of pork at a time and remove them with a draining spoon to paper towels. Continue until all the pork is fried.

3. Pour off most of the oil from the wok and add the sliced onion, pepper and pineapple. Cook over high heat for 1-2 minutes. Remove and set aside.

4. Mix all the sauce ingredients together and pour into the wok. Bring slowly to the boil, stirring continuously until thickened. Allow to simmer for about 1-2 minutes or until completely clear.

5. Add the vegetables, pineapple and pork cubes to the sauce and stir to coat completely. Reheat for 1-2 minutes and serve immediately.

TIME: Preparation takes about 15 minutes, cooking takes about 15 minutes.

VARIATION: Use beef or chicken instead of the pork. Uncooked, peeled shrimp may be used as can whitefish, cut into 1-inch pieces.

SPICED BEEF

A classic recipe which requires the best-quality beef.

SERVES 2-3

Marinade
1 tsp sugar
2-3 star anise, ground
½ tsp ground fennel
1 tbsp dark soy sauce
¼ tsp monosodium glutamate (optional)

1lb fillet of beef, cut into 1-inch strips
1 inch fresh root ginger, peeled and
   crushed
½ tsp salt
2 tbsps oil
4 green onions, sliced
½ tsp freshly ground black pepper
1 tbsp light soy sauce

1. Mix the marinade ingredients together.

2. Add the beef strips, ginger and salt, and marinate for 20 minutes.

3. Heat the oil in wok and stir-fry the onions for 1 minute.

4. Add the beef, ground pepper and soy sauce and stir-fry for 4-5 minutes.

TIME: Preparation takes 30 minutes, cooking takes 5-6 minutes.

COOK'S TIP: Fresh root ginger keeps well if wrapped in food wrap and stored in the refrigerator.

MEAT AND SHRIMP CHOW MEIN

*This chow mein is a wonderful mix
of vegetables, meat and seafood.*

SERVES 4

1lb dried Chinese noodles or broken
   spaghetti
¼ cup oil
2-3 green onions, chopped
4oz cooked ham, shredded
¾ cup peeled shrimp
4oz shredded carrots
4oz green beans, sliced
Salt to taste
1 tsp sugar
1 tbsp rice wine or dry sherry
4oz cooked chicken, shredded
2 cups bean sprouts
2½ tbsps soy sauce

1. Cook the noodles in boiling, salted water for 4-5 minutes. Rinse under cold water and drain thoroughly.

2. Toss in 1 tbsp oil. Heat the remaining oil in a wok.

3. Add the onions, ham, shrimp, carrots and green beans and stir-fry for 2-3 minutes.

4. Add the salt, sugar, wine, chicken and bean sprouts. Cook for 2 minutes.

5. Add the cooked noodles and soy sauce. Cook for 1-2 minutes. Serve immediately.

TIME: Preparation takes 20 minutes, cooking takes 12-15 minutes.

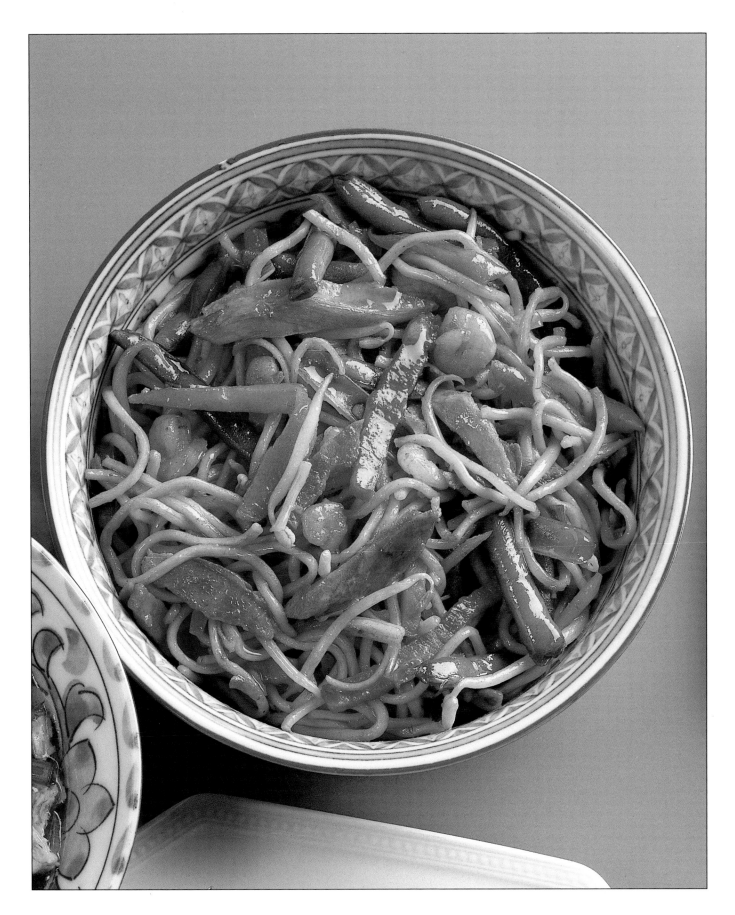

Sweet and Sour Pork and Pineapple

*Sweet and sour recipes are perfect for mixed
gatherings as children often enjoy them as much as adults.*

SERVES 4

1lb lean pork fillet, cut into
   1-inch cubes
2 tbsps light soy sauce
2 tbsps white wine vinegar
2 tbsps tomato paste
1 tbsp sugar
2 tbsps peanut oil
1 tbsp cornstarch
1 clove garlic, crushed
1 tsp grated root ginger
½ cup water
1 can pineapple pieces, drained
Fresh Chinese parsley (cilantro) to garnish

1. Place pork in bowl. Pour over light soy sauce and toss together. Leave for 15 minutes.

2. Mix together vinegar, tomato paste and sugar, and set aside.

3. Heat wok and add oil. Remove pork from soy sauce, and add soy sauce to sauce mixture.

4. Toss pork in cornstarch, coating well. When oil is hot, brown pork well all over.

5. Remove from pan and reduce heat. Fry garlic and ginger for 30 seconds.

6. Add water. Bring to the boil, then return pork to wok. Reduce heat, cover and simmer for 15 minutes, stirring occasionally.

7. Add sauce mixture and pineapple, and simmer for a further 15 minutes. Garnish with Chinese parsley.

TIME: Preparation takes 20 minutes, cooking takes 45 minutes.

SERVING IDEA: Serve with rice or noodles.

STIR-FRY BEEF WITH MANGO SLICES

This oriental combination of ingredients is refreshingly different.

SERVES 2-3

½lb fillet of beef
1 tbsp cooking wine
1 tbsp soy sauce
1 tsp cornstarch
¼ tsp sugar
¼ tsp pepper
1 large mango
4 tbsps oil
1 tbsp shredded ginger root
1 tbsp shredded green onions

1. Cut beef into thin bite-sized slices. Marinate in the wine, soy sauce, cornstarch, sugar and pepper for 20 minutes.

2. Skin mango, cut into ¼-inch thick slices.

3. Set wok over a high heat, pour 4 tbsps oil into the wok, wait until it's almost smoking. Reduce heat to moderate, stir-fry the beef and ginger for 1-2 minutes. Remove with a slotted spoon.

4. Toss the mango slices in the hot oil for a few seconds, return the beef and ginger, and green onions. Stir over the heat for a further few seconds. Serve immediately.

TIME: Preparation takes 30 minutes, cooking takes about 3 minutes.

COOK'S TIP: If you cannot get a fresh mango – canned mango is available from supermarkets.

LAMB MEATBALLS WITH YOGURT

A refreshing recipe which will have everyone asking for more.

SERVES 3-4

1lb lean ground lamb
2 cloves garlic, crushed
1 small onion, peeled and grated
½ tsp chili powder
1 tsp garam masala
1 tbsp chopped mint
1oz breadcrumbs
1 egg, lightly beaten
Salt
Pepper
2 tbsps oil
Small pinch of salmon strands, or ¼ tsp
    ground turmeric
2 tbsps boiling water
5 tbsps natural yogurt
Fresh Chinese parsley (cilantro) or mint to
    garnish

1. In a bowl, mix together ground lamb,
garlic, onion, chili powder, garam masala,
mint and breadcrumbs.

2. Add lightly beaten egg to bind
ingredients together. Add salt and pepper
to taste.

3. Wet hands. Take a teaspoon of mixture,
and roll between palms, forming small
balls.

4. Heat wok and add oil. Add meatballs,
shake wok to make meatballs roll around,
and fry until browned well all over.

5. Add saffron or turmeric to 2 tbsps
boiling water. Leave for 5 minutes.

6. Add water to yogurt, and stir in until
evenly mixed. Reheat meatballs and serve
on yogurt.

7. Garnish with mint or fresh cilantro.
Serve with rice.

TIME: Preparation takes 15 minutes, cooking takes 30 minutes.

COOK'S TIP: Saffron is expensive, so if you do not intend to use it very
often it may be better to use turmeric.

CARAMELIZED SPARERIBS

*These sweet, caramelized spareribs are always a
success. Tell guests to use their fingers; knives
or chopsticks are out of the question.*

SERVES 4

1 carrot
1 bay leaf
1 leek
2lbs pork spareribs, separated
1 tbsp.honey
1 tbsp white wine vinegar
1 tsp chopped garlic
2 tbsps soy sauce
⅓ cup chicken stock
Salt and pepper

1. In a large saucepan combine 4 cups
water with the carrot, bay leaf and leek.
Bring to the boil and add the spareribs.
Blanch the meat for 10 minutes, remove
from the stock and drain well.

2. Lay the ribs in an ovenproof pan.
Combine the honey, vinegar and garlic,
and spread the mixture on the ribs.

3. Add the soy sauce and the stock to the
dish. Season well with salt and pepper.

4. Put into a very hot oven, 475°F, and
cook until the ribs are caramelized and
have turned a rich, dark brown color.

TIME: Preparation takes about 5 minutes and cooking takes approximately
55 minutes, from start to finish.

SERVING IDEA: Serve on a bed of finely shredded lettuce leaves, lightly
seasoned with salt and pepper.

PEKING BEEF

In China, meat is often simmered in large earthenware
casseroles, but a wok is a convenient substitute.

SERVES 8

2lb roast of beef
1¾ cups white wine
2½ cups water
2 whole green onions, roots trimmed
1-inch piece fresh ginger
3 star anise
2 tsps sugar
½ cup soy sauce
1 carrot, peeled
2 sticks celery
½ mooli (daikon) radish, peeled

1. Place the beef in a wok and add the white wine, water, green onions, ginger and anise. Cover and simmer for about 1 hour.

2. Add the sugar and soy sauce, stir and simmer for 30 minutes longer, or until the beef is tender. Allow to cool in the liquid.

3. Shred all the vegetables finely. Blanch them all, except the green onion, in boiling water for about 1 minute. Rinse under cold water, drain and leave to dry.

4. When the meat is cold, remove it from the liquid and cut into thin slices. Arrange on a serving plate and strain the liquid over it. Scatter over the shredded vegetables and serve cold.

TIME: Preparation takes about 25 minutes if shredding the vegetables by hand. This can also be done with the fine shredding blade of a food processor. Cooking takes about 1½ hours.

ECONOMY: Because of the long cooking time, less expensive cuts of meat may be used for this dish.

COOK'S TIP: If using a rolled roast, remove as much of the fat from the outside as possible. Skim off any fat that rises to the surface of the liquid as it cools, before pouring over the meat to serve.

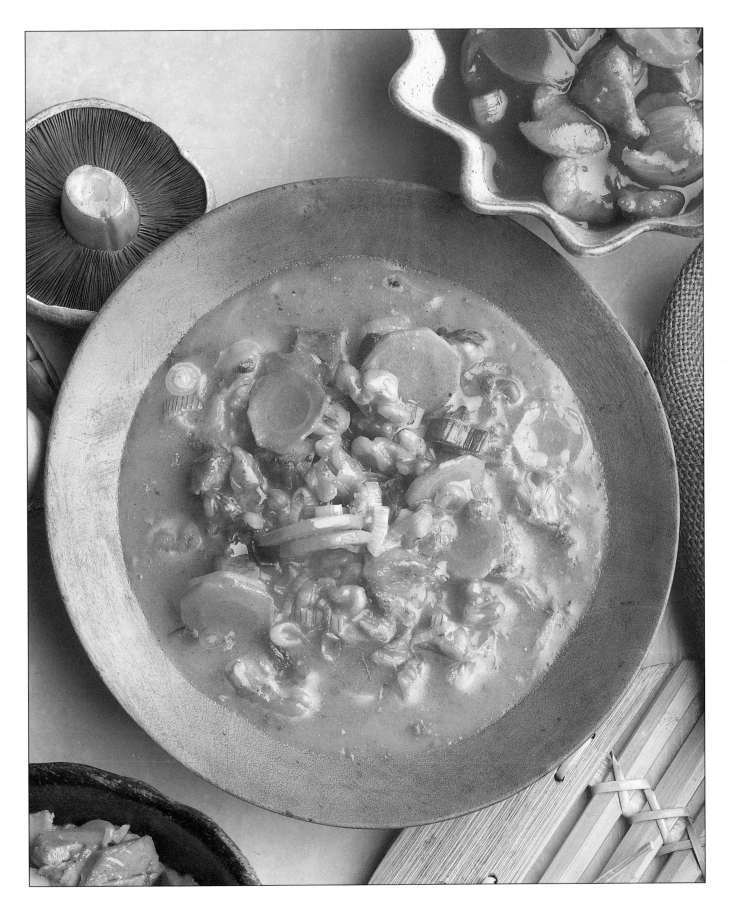

BEEF WITH TOMATO AND PEPPER IN BLACK BEAN SAUCE

*Black beans are a specialty of Cantonese cooking and give
a pungent, salty taste to stir-fried dishes.*

SERVES 6

2 large tomatoes
2 tbsps salted black beans
2 tbsps water
4 tbsps dark soy sauce
1 tbsp cornstarch
1 tbsp dry sherry
1 tsp sugar
1lb rump steak, cut into thin strips
1 small green pepper, seeded and cored
4 tbsps oil
¾ cup beef stock
Pinch pepper

1. Core tomatoes and cut them into 16 wedges. Crush the black beans, add the water and set aside.

2. Combine soy sauce, cornstarch, sherry, sugar and meat in a bowl and set aside.

3. Cut pepper into ½-inch diagonal pieces. Heat the wok and add the oil. When hot, stir-fry the green pepper pieces for about 1 minute and remove.

4. Add the meat and the soy sauce mixture to the wok and stir-fry for about 2 minutes. Add the soaked black beans and the stock. Bring to the boil and allow to thicken slightly. Return the peppers to the wok and add the tomatoes and pepper. Heat through for 1 minute and serve immediately.

TIME: Preparation takes about 25 minutes, cooking takes about 5 minutes.

SERVING IDEA: Serve with plain boiled rice.

WATCHPOINT: Do not add the tomatoes too early or stir the mixture too vigorously once they are added or they will fall apart.

VARIATION: Substitute snow peas for the green peppers in the recipe. Mushrooms may also be added and cooked with the pepper or snow peas.

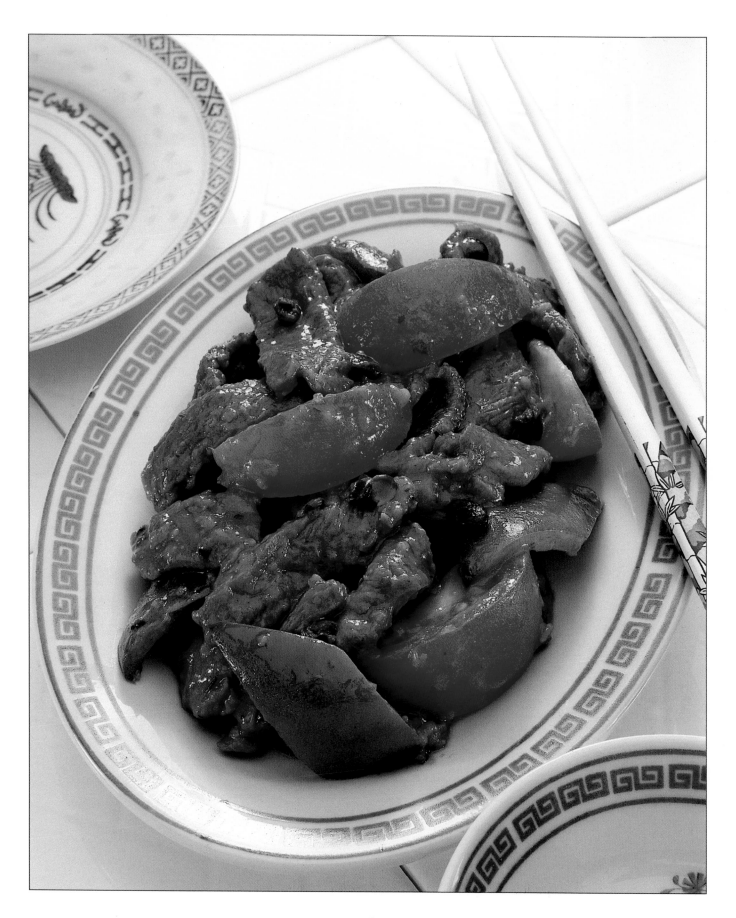

STEAMED LAMB WITH MUSHROOM SAUCE

A great combination that should please most appetites.

SERVES 4-6

2¼lbs boned leg of lamb, cut
   into strips
2 green onions, thinly sliced
Salt and freshly ground black pepper
2 tsps oil
2 cloves of garlic, peeled and sliced
1 tsp cornstarch
Pinch monosodium glutamate (optional)
5 tbsps light soy sauce
3 tbsps rice wine or dry sherry
1 tsp crushed black pepper
1 inch fresh root ginger, peeled and
   thinly sliced
1 cup sliced mushrooms
Few drops sesame oil

1. Put the lamb into a saucepan and add sufficient water to cover. Boil 5 minutes. Drain the lamb and retain the water. Arrange lamb strips in a deep dish and sprinkle the green onions on top. Season with pepper and salt.

2. Heat the oil in a wok and fry the garlic until brown. Remove the garlic and discard.

3. Mix together the cornstarch, monosodium glutamate, soy sauce, wine, crushed pepper, ginger and 4 tbsps reserved water.

4. Stir the cornstarch mixture into the oil in the wok, add the mushrooms and cook for 1-2 minutes. Pour over the lamb.

5. Cover the lamb with overlapping foil and tie around the rim. Put the dish in a steamer and steam over boiling water for 2 hours. Serve with the sesame oil sprinkled over the lamb.

TIME: Preparation takes 20-25 minutes, cooking takes 2 hours 10 minutes.

CHICKEN AND BEAN SPROUT SALAD

Steamed chicken and bean sprouts, coated in a refreshingly light sauce.

SERVES 4

3 cups bean sprouts
12oz chicken breast meat
1 tbsp soy sauce
2 tbsps chopped chives
1 tbsp white wine vinegar
1 tsp sugar
1 tbsp soy sauce
Pinch chopped garlic
1 tbsp peanut oil
½ tsp sesame oil
Salt and pepper

1. Cook the bean sprouts for 2 minutes in boiling water. Drain and refresh under cold water. Set aside to drain completely.

2. Sprinkle the chicken with 1 tsp soy sauce and cook in a Chinese steamer.

3. Once the chicken is cooked, set it aside to cool and then slice thinly.

4. Prepare the sauce by mixing together the remaining ingredients and seasoning with a little salt and pepper. Allow the sauce to stand for 20 minutes.

5. Mix together the bean sprouts and the chicken. Pour over the sauce and serve.

TIME: Preparation takes about 15 minutes and cooking also takes about 15 minutes.

VARIATION: The chicken could be cooked in stock, to which the soy sauce has been added.

COOK'S TIP: Mix together the sauce ingredients the day before using them.
The flavors will have more time to develop fully.

ROAST CRISPY DUCK

This dish can be served as a main course for 4 or as an appetizer for 6.

SERVES 4-6

4½lbs duck or goose, prepared for
  cooking
4 tbsps maltose or corn syrup
1 cup water
12 green onions, cut into 2-inch lengths
½ tsp red food coloring
2 tbsps tomato paste

Duck Dip
½ cup sugar
4 tbsps sweet bean paste
2 tbsps sesame oil
½ cup water

1. Wash the duck and pat it dry on a clean cloth. Ease the finger between the skin and flesh of the duck, starting at the neck end and working the length of the bird. Put a stick or large skewer through the neck and the cavity of the duck to wedge it securely. This will make the duck easier to handle. Hold the duck over the sink and pour boiling water all over it. Pat the duck dry.

2. Melt half the maltose and dissolve in the water. Stand the duck on a rack over a deep tray. Slowly pour the maltose liquid over the duck. Pour the maltose liquid over the duck 3 or 4 times. Leave the duck in a cool place for 6-8 hours, or overnight, until the skin is dry.

3. Remove the skewer. Stand the duck on a rack in a roasting pan. Preheat the oven to 400°F and cook for 30 minutes. Turn over and cook the underside for a further 30 minutes.

4. Melt the remaining maltose with the tomato paste and add the food coloring. Spread over the duck and cook for a further 30 minutes. (The duck should have a crisp, redish-brown skin.)

5. Heat the wok and add the mixed ingredients for the duck dip. Cook for 3-4 minutes until the sugar has dissolved and the dip is smooth. Serve in individual cups.

6. Remove the duck skin in squares. Slice the duck flesh and serve with the skin on top.

TIME: Preparation takes 15-20 minutes, plus 6-8 hours to dry, cooking takes 1 hour 30 minutes.

TANGERINE PEEL CHICKEN

*An exotic mixture of flavors blend perfectly
in this delicious chicken dish.*

SERVES 2

1lb boned chicken breast, cut into 1-inch
  pieces

Seasoning
½ tsp salt
1½ tsps sugar
½ tsp monosodium glutamate (optional)
1 tsp dark soy sauce
2 tsps light soy sauce
1 tsp rice wine or dry sherry
2 tsps malt vinegar
1 tsp sesame oil
2 tsps cornstarch

Oil for deep frying
1-2 red or green chilies, chopped
½ inch fresh root ginger, peeled and
  finely chopped
2 inches dried tangerine peel, coarsely
  ground or crumbled
2 green onions, finely chopped

Sauce
½ tsp cornstarch
1-2 tbsps water or stock

1. Mix the chicken pieces with the seasoning ingredients and stir well. Leave to marinate for 10-15 minutes. Remove the chicken pieces and reserve the marinade.

2. Heat wok and add the oil for deep frying. Once it starts to smoke add the chicken pieces and fry for 4-5 minutes until golden. Drain chicken on paper towels.

3. Pour off the oil, leaving 1 tbsp oil in the wok, and stir-fry the chilies, ginger, tangerine peel and onions for 2-3 minutes. When they begin to color add the chicken and stir-fry for 1 minute.

4. Mix the reserved marinade with the sauce ingredients and pour over the chicken. Stir and cook for 2-3 minutes until the sauce thickens and the chicken is tender. Serve immediately.

TIME: Preparation takes 30 minutes, cooking takes 12-15 minutes.

CHICKEN IN HOT PEPPER SAUCE

Stir-fried chicken served with peppers in a hot sauce.

SERVES 4

1 chicken
2 tbsps oil
1 tsp chopped garlic
1 green pepper, seeded and cut into thin
    strips
1 red pepper, seeded and cut into thin
    strips
1 tsp wine vinegar
1 tbsp light soy sauce
1 tsp sugar
1⅓ cups chicken stock
1 tbsp chili sauce
Salt and pepper

1. First, bone the chicken. To bone the legs, cut down along the bone on all sides, drawing out the bone with an even movement. Cut all the chicken meat into thin strips.

2. Heat the oil in a wok and stir-fry the garlic, chicken and the green and red peppers.

3. Pour off any excess oil and deglaze the wok with the vinegar. Stir in the soy sauce, sugar and stock.

4. Gradually stir in the chili sauce, tasting after each addition. Season with a little salt and pepper to taste.

5. Cook until the sauce has reduced slightly. Serve piping hot.

TIME: Preparation takes 10 minutes and cooking takes approximately 25 minutes.

Sliced Duck with Bamboo Shoots and Broccoli

*A delightful recipe which mixes some of
China's best-loved ingredients.*

SERVES 2

2¼lb small duck
1 tsp monosodium glutamate (optional)
2½ tsps cornstarch
2 tbsps water
4oz broccoli, chopped
3 tbsps oil
2-3 green onions, chopped
1 inch fresh root ginger, peeled and
    thinly sliced
1 clove garlic, peeled and finely chopped
4oz bamboo shoots, sliced
½ tsp sugar
Salt and freshly ground black pepper to
    taste
¼ cup chicken stock
2 tsps rice wine or sweet sherry
Few drops sesame oil

1. Cut the duck flesh into bite-size pieces,
removing all the bones.

2. Mix the the monosodium glutamate,
1½ tsps cornstarch and 1 tbsp water
together. Stir into the duck. Marinate for
20 minutes.

3. Cook the broccoli in boiling water for 1
minute. Drain thoroughly.

4. Heat the wok and add the oil. Stir-fry
the onions, ginger, garlic and bamboo
shoots for 1-2 minutes.

5. Add the duck pieces and stir-fry for 2-3
minutes. Add the sugar, salt and pepper to
taste, stock, rice wine, sesame oil and
broccoli. Stir-fry for 3 minutes.

6. Add the remaining cornstarch and water
blended together. Stir over the heat until
the sauce thickens. Serve immediately.

COOK'S TIP: Fresh root ginger keeps well if tightly wrapped in
plastic wrap and stored in the refrigerator.

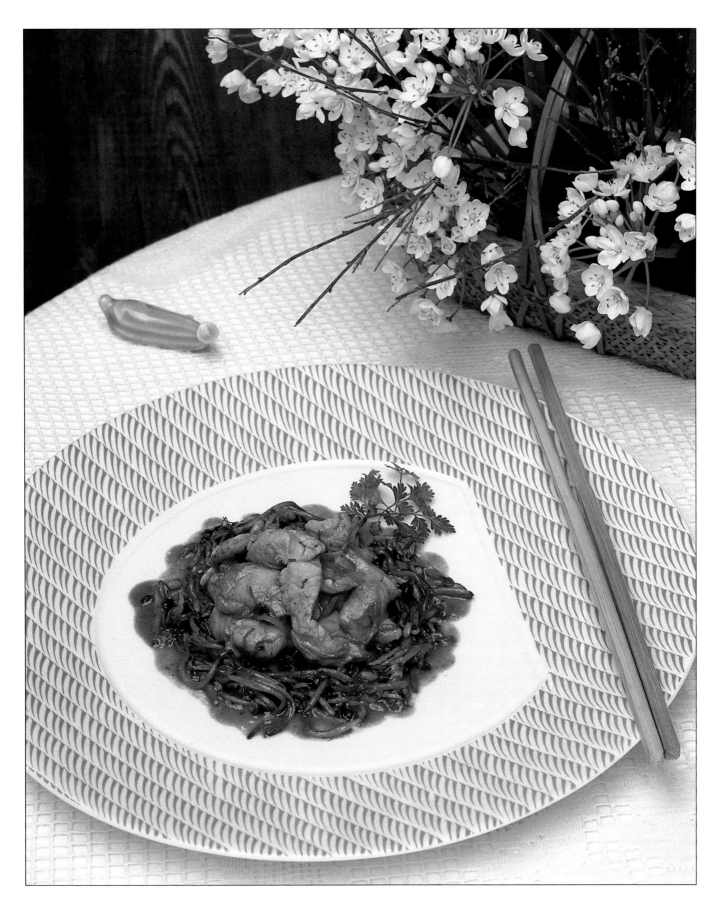

CHICKEN AND MUSHROOMS

A classic combination which always tastes great.

SERVES 2

Seasoning
½ tsp salt
2 tbsps light soy sauce
2 tsps cornstarch
1 tsp rice wine or dry sherry
Pinch monosodium glutamate (optional)

½lb chicken breast, cut into bite-size pieces

Sauce
Salt to taste
Freshly ground black pepper to taste
1 tbsp light soy sauce
1 cup chicken stock
2 tsps cornstarch or arrowroot
1 tsp oyster sauce

2 tbsps oil
1 onion, peeled and chopped
1 clove of garlic, sliced
½ inch fresh root ginger, peeled and
   thinly sliced
3 dried black mushrooms, soaked and
   sliced
2oz open mushrooms, sliced
2oz button mushrooms, sliced

1. Mix the seasoning ingredients together. Marinate the chicken in the seasoning mixture for 10 minutes.

2. Mix the sauce ingredients together.

3. Heat the oil in a wok and fry the onion, garlic and ginger for 2-3 minutes. Remove and put to one side.

4. Fry the drained chicken in the remaining oil for 4 minutes.

5. Add the mushrooms and stir-fry for 1 minute. Add a little extra oil if necessary.

6. Return the fried onion mixture to the wok and stir-fry until well mixed. Pour the blended sauce ingredients into the wok and cook gently until the sauce thickens. Serve piping hot.

TIME: Preparation takes 15 minutes, plus 10 minutes to marinate. Cooking takes 10-12 minutes.

COOK'S TIP: Supermarkets now have a wider range of mushrooms so choose your favorites if you cannot get those in the recipe.

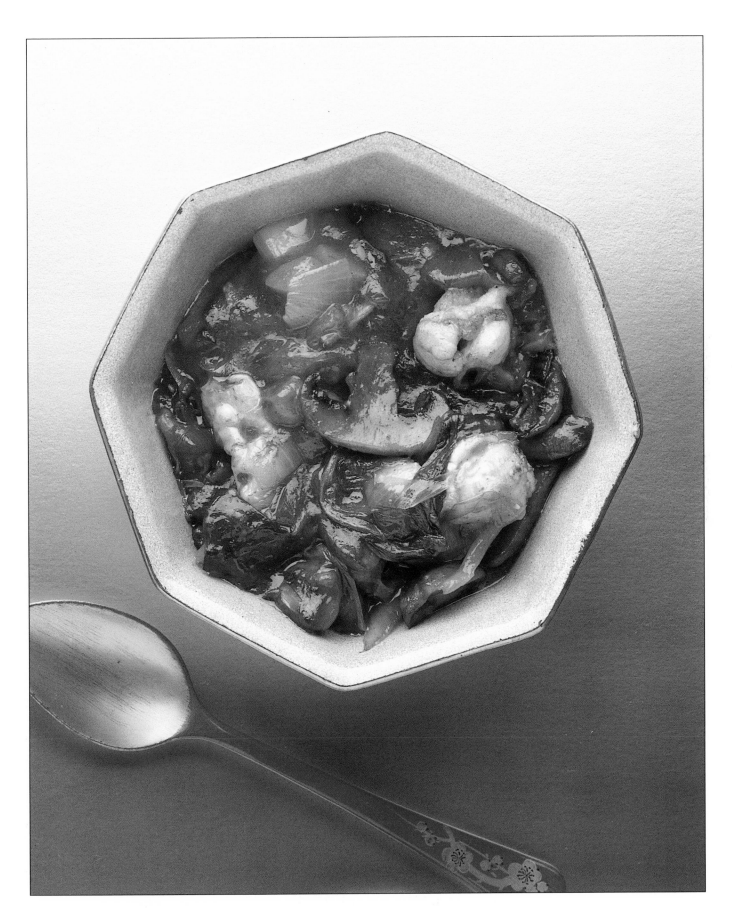

DUCK WITH BAMBOO SHOOTS

Stir-fried bamboo shoots, served with duck breasts and Hoisin-based sauce.

SERVES 4

4oz bamboo shoots, cut into thin slices
¼ cup sugar
⅓ cup water
1 tsp chopped fresh ginger root
1 tbsp Hoisin sauce
2 duck breasts
1 tbsp oil
Salt and pepper

---

1. Cook the bamboo shoots in boiling, lightly salted water for approximately 15 minutes. Drain thoroughly and set aside.

2. Mix the sugar and water together in a small saucepan, stirring thoroughly.

3. Add the ginger and the Hoisin sauce. Place over a gentle heat and cook until a light syrup is formed.

4. Brush this syrup over the duck breasts.

5. Heat the oil in a frying pan and add the duck breasts, skin-side down first. Sear on each side. Take out and finish cooking in a hot oven, 425°F, for approximately 15 minutes.

6. Shortly before the duck breasts are cooked, stir-fry the bamboo shoots in the oil used to sear the duck breasts. Season with salt and pepper and serve hot with the sliced duck breasts.

TIME: Preparation takes about 10 minutes and total cooking time is approximately 50 minutes.

SERVING IDEA: Serve any leftover sauce in a small bowl to accompany the duck.

WATCHPOINT: Don't forget to begin searing the meat in the frying pan skin-side down and then finish with the other side.

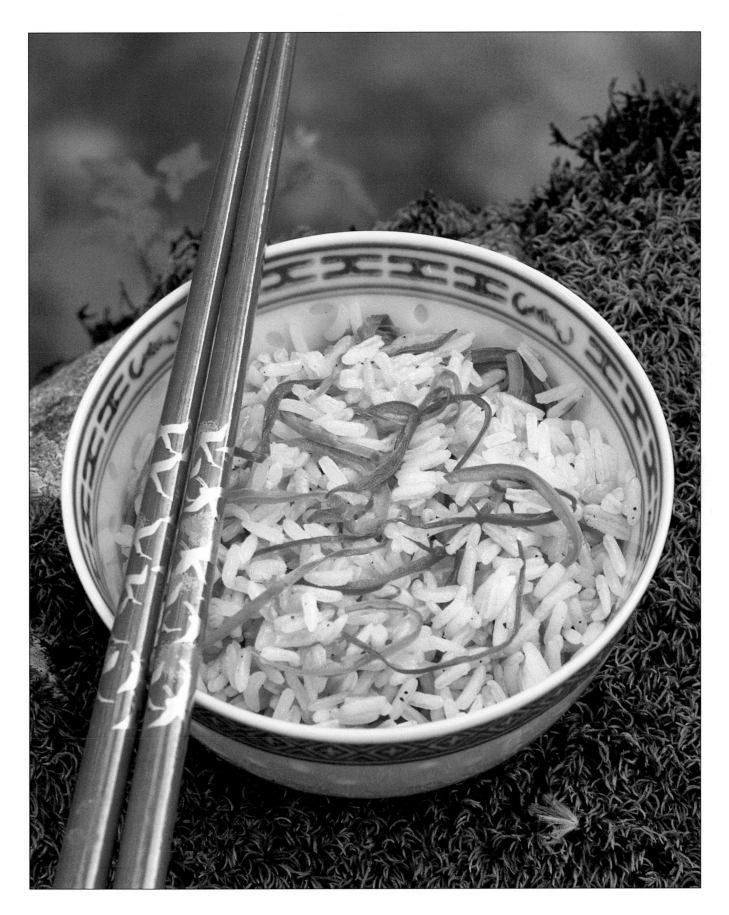

FRIED VEGETABLES WITH GINGER

*Use your imagination with this recipe and adapt it
to whatever greens you can buy.*

SERVES 4-6

2¼lbs mixed Chinese green vegetables
(cabbage, spinach, kale, broccoli,
Chinese leaf etc.)
2oz snow peas
1 tsp baking soda
2 tsps sugar
1 tsp salt
2 tbsps oil
1 inch fresh root ginger, peeled and
shredded
1 green pepper, seeded and diced
1 green or red chili, sliced into strips

Sauce
2 tsps dark soy sauce
1 tsp sugar
1 cup chicken stock
2 tsps cornstarch
1 tsp five spice powder

To Serve
½ tsp sesame oil
Freshly ground black pepper to taste

1. Cut greens into 3-inch pieces. Bring a large pan of water to the boil and add the sugar and salt.

2. Add the snow peas and greens and cook for 4-5 minutes. Drain green vegetables and discard water.

3. Add 1 tbsp oil to the vegetables and keep covered. Heat the remaining oil in the wok and stir fry the ginger for 1 minute.

4. Add the green pepper and chilies and stir-fry for 10-12 minutes. Add the blended sauce ingredients and stir well. Simmer gently for 3-4 minutes.

5. Add the green vegetables and cook for 1 minute. Serve immediately, sprinkled with sesame oil and pepper.

TIME: Preparation takes 10 minutes, cooking takes 13-15 minutes.

PLAIN FRIED RICE

*Producing perfect rice is a must
for lovers of Chinese food.*

SERVES

1lb long grain rice
¼ tsp monosodium glutamate
2 tbsps oil
Salt

1. Wash the rice in 4-5 changes of cold water. Drain the rice and put into a large pan or wok. Add sufficient cold water to come 1-inch above the level of the rice. Bring to the boil.

2. Stir once and reduce the heat to simmer. Cover and cook gently for 5-7 minutes until the water has been totally absorbed and the rice is separate and fluffy, with the necessary amount of stickiness to be handled by chopsticks.

3. Spread the rice out on a tray to cool. Sprinkle with the monosodium glutamate. Heat the oil in wok or large frying pan and add the rice. Stir fry for 1-2 minutes.

4. Add salt to taste and stir-fry for a further 1-2 minutes.

TIME: Preparation takes 5 minutes, plus cooling time, cooking takes 10-11 minutes.

SZECHUAN EGGPLANT

An unusual side-dish which adds extra spice to meals.

SERVES 2

Oil
1 large eggplant cut into 2-inch long and
    ½-inch thick strips
3 cloves garlic, peeled and finely sliced
1 inch fresh root ginger, peeled and
    shredded
1 onion, peeled and finely chopped
2 green onions, chopped
4oz cooked and shredded chicken
1 red or green chili, cut into strips

Seasoning
½ cup chicken stock
1 tsp sugar
1 tsp red vinegar or wine vinegar
½ tsp salt
½ tsp freshly ground black pepper

Sauce
1 tsp cornstarch
1 tbsp water
1 tsp sesame oil

1. Heat the wok and add 3 tbsps oil. Add eggplant and stir-fry for 4-5 minutes. The eggplant will absorb a lot of oil; keep stirring or else they will burn. Remove from wok and put to one side.

2. Heat the wok and add 2 tbsps oil. Add the garlic and ginger and fry for 1 minute.

3. Add the onions and fry for 2 minutes. Add the chicken and chili. Cook for 1 minute.

4. Return the eggplants to the wok. Add the blended seasoning ingredients and simmer for 6-7 minutes.

5. Stir in the blended sauce ingredients and simmer until the sauce thickens. Serve with extra sesame oil if desired.

TIME: Preparation takes 15 minutes, cooking takes 18-20 minutes.

COOK'S TIP: Vary the spiciness of this dish by increasing the quantity of chilies.

STIR-FRIED CHINESE CABBAGE

Stir-fried Chinese cabbage, zucchini and pepper,
flavored with sesame oil and soy sauce.

SERVES 4

1 head Chinese cabbage
2 zucchini
2 tbsps oil
1 tsp chopped garlic
1 tbsp chopped red pepper
1 tbsp soy sauce
Salt and pepper
Few drops sesame oil

1. Shred the Chinese cabbage quite finely.

2. Prepare the zucchini, first topping and tailing them and then slicing down the sides, preserving a bit of the flesh with the peel. Slice finely.

3. Heat the oil in a wok, add the Chinese cabbage and garlic and stir-fry for 2 minutes.

4. Add the zucchini, hot red pepper, soy sauce, salt and pepper. Continue cooking for 3 minutes and serve hot with the sesame oil drizzled on top.

TIME: Preparation takes about 10 minutes and cooking takes approximately 5 minutes.

VARIATION: If you like hot, spicy dishes, add ¼ tsp chili sauce to the Chinese cabbage.

SERVING IDEA: Cooked in this way, the Chinese cabbage will remain crisp.
If you prefer, cook longer for a softer texture.

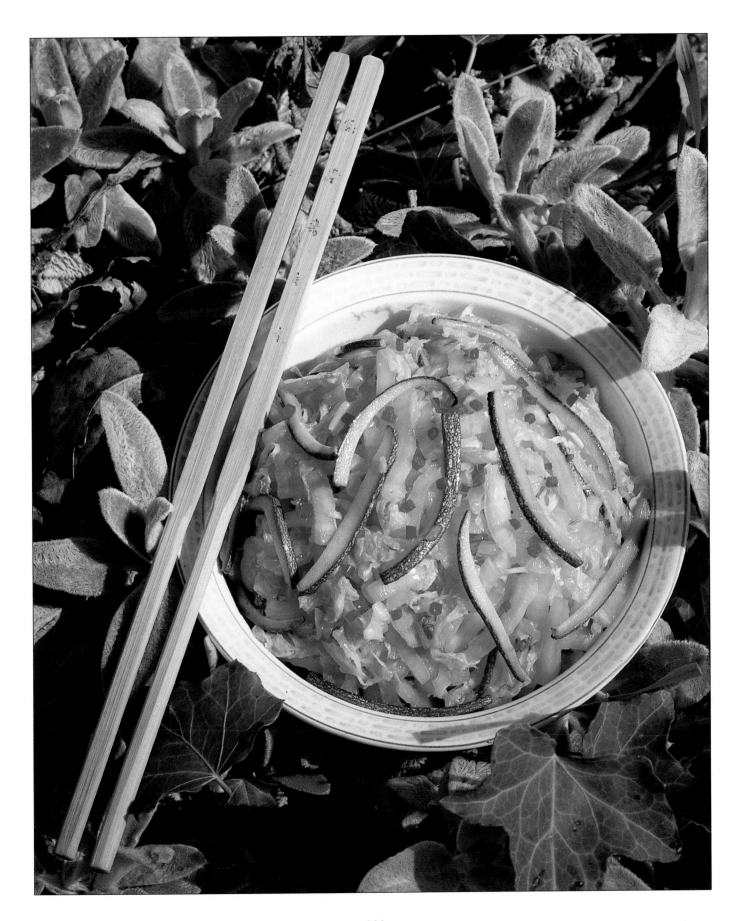

FRIED RICE

*A basic recipe for a traditional Chinese accompaniment to
stir-fried dishes, this can be more substantial with the
addition of meat, poultry or seafood.*

SERVES 6-8

1lb cooked rice, well drained and dried
3 tbsps oil
1 egg, beaten
1 tbsp soy sauce
½ cup cooked peas
Dash sesame oil
Salt and pepper
2 green onions, thinly sliced

1. Heat a wok and add the oil. Pour in the
egg and soy sauce and cook until just
beginning to set.

2. Add the rice and peas and stir to coat
with the egg mixture. Allow to cook for
about 3 minutes, stirring continuously.
Add seasoning and sesame oil.

3. Spoon into a serving dish and sprinkle
over the green onions.

TIME: The rice will take about 10 minutes to cook. Allow at least 20 minutes for it to drain
as dry as possible. The fried rice dish will take about 4 minutes to cook.

VARIATION: Cooked meat, poultry or seafood may be added to the rice along with the peas.

COOK'S TIP: The 1lb rice measurement is the cooked weight.

VEGETABLE STIR-FRY

A marvellous blend of Chinese vegetables and nuts,
stir-fried in a little oil and then cooked in an aromatic sauce.

SERVES 4

2 dried lotus roots, soaked overnight in
   water
2 tbsps oil
1½ cups bean sprouts
½ red pepper, seeded and finely chopped
½ green pepper, seeded and finely
   chopped
½ green onion, chopped
1 head Chinese cabbage, finely chopped
3oz dried Chinese black mushrooms,
   soaked for 1 hour in warm water
1 zucchini thinly sliced
¾ cup frozen peas
2 tbsps cashew nuts, roughly chopped
1 tsp sugar
2 tbsps soy sauce
1¾ cups chicken stock
Salt and pepper

1. Cook the lotus roots in boiling, lightly salted water for 20 minutes. Slice thinly.

2. Heat the oil in a wok and stir-fry, in the following order, the bean sprouts, peppers, onion, Chinese cabbage, lotus root, mushrooms, zucchini, peas and cashew nuts.

3. Stir in the sugar, soy sauce and stock.

4. Season with salt and pepper and cook for 30 minutes, stirring frequently.

5. Serve the vegetables slightly drained of the sauce.

TIME: Preparation takes about 10 minutes and cooking takes approximately 35 minutes.

VARIATION: Any type of nut could be used in this recipe, for example walnuts, hazelnuts or almonds.

COOK'S TIP: If time permits, this recipe is even more delicious if the vegetables are stir-fried separately, each cooked vegetable being removed from the wok before continuing with the next. Finish by cooking all the vegetables together for 30 minutes in the chicken stock as above.

SPECIAL MIXED VEGETABLES

This dish illustrates the basic stir-frying technique for vegetables.

SERVES 4

1 tbsp oil
1 clove garlic, crushed
1-inch piece fresh ginger, sliced
4 Chinese cabbage leaves, shredded
2oz flat mushrooms, thinly sliced
2oz bamboo shoots, sliced
3 sticks celery, diagonally sliced
2oz baby corn, cut in half if large
1 small red pepper, cored, seeded and
    thinly sliced
1 cup bean sprouts
Salt and pepper
2 tbsps light soy sauce
Dash sesame oil
3 tomatoes, peeled, seeded and quartered

1. Heat the oil in a wok and add the ingredients in the order given, reserving the soy sauce, sesame oil and tomatoes.

2. To make it easier to peel the tomatoes, remove the stems and place in boiling water for 5 seconds.

3. Remove from the boiling water with a draining spoon and place in a bowl of cold water. This will make the peels easier to remove. Cut out the core end using a small sharp knife.

4. Cut the tomatoes in half and then in quarters. Use a teaspoon or a serrated edged knife to remove the seeds and the cores.

5. Cook the vegetables for about 2 minutes. Stir in the soy sauce and sesame oil and add the tomatoes. Heat through for 30 seconds and serve immediately.

TIME: Preparation takes about 25 minutes, cooking takes about 2-3 minutes.

VARIATION: Other vegetables such as broccoli florets, cauliflower florets, snow peas, zucchini or French beans may be used.

SERVING IDEA: Serve as a side dish or as a vegetarian main dish with plain or fried rice.

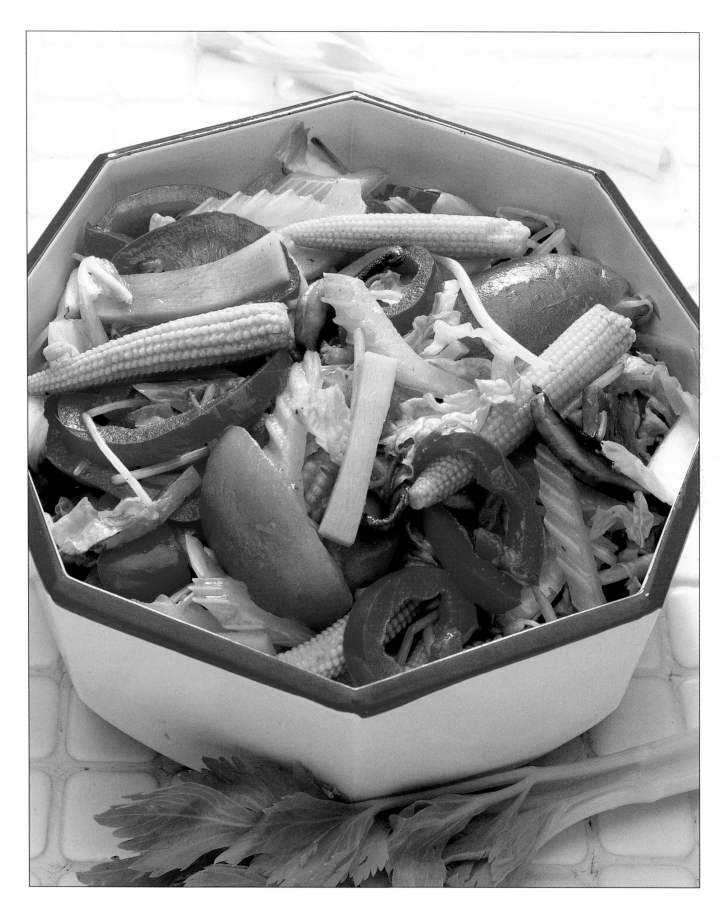

SWEET AND SOUR CABBAGE

A tasty combination which suits cabbage perfectly.

SERVES 4

1lb white cabbage, shredded
½ tsp baking soda
1 tsp salt
2 tsps sugar
1 tbsp oil

Sauce
2 tbsps sugar
2 tbsps wine vinegar
1 cup chicken stock or water
Pinch of salt
1 tbsp cornstarch
Few drops red food coloring
1 tsp tomato paste

1. Boil the cabbage in a large pan of water with the baking soda, salt and sugar for 2-3 minutes. Drain the cabbage and discard the boiling water.

2. Keep the cabbage in cold water for 5 minutes. Drain and keep on one side.

3. Heat the wok and add the oil. Fry the cabbage until it is heated through. Remove on to a serving dish.

4. Combine the sauce ingredients, stir well, add to the wok and gently bring to the boil, stirring. Stir over the heat until the sauce thickens. Pour over the cabbage and serve immediately.

TIME: Preparation takes 10 minutes, cooking takes 10 minutes.

COOK'S TIP: The red food coloring is optional as it only accentuates the color.

Microwave

Chicken Corn Chowder with Almonds
Shrimp and Lettuce Soup
Soup of Mushrooms and Peas
Shanghai Noodle Snack
Ham and Bean Fried Rice
Embroidered Crabmeat Balls
Shrimp with Baby Corn
Scallops in Pepper Sauce
Beef with Green Pepper, Tomato
and Black Beans
Szechuan Beef
Singapore Chicken
Chicken with Snow Peas
Duck with Pineapple
Empress Chicken
Chicken with Hoisin Sauce and Cashews
Sweet-Sour Cabbage
Ten Varieties of Beauty
Beans with Bamboo Shoots
Spicy Cucumbers
Ginger Broccoli

CHICKEN CORN CHOWDER WITH ALMONDS

Toasted almonds add a special flavor to this chowder.

SERVES 4

2 x 8oz cans creamed corn
1 quart chicken stock
2 chicken breasts, finely chopped
2 tbsps cornstarch
2 tbsps rice wine
½ cup toasted almonds
Salt and pepper

1. Combine corn, stock and chicken in a large deep bowl.

2. Partially cover and cook 3-5 minutes or until chicken is nearly cooked.

3. Combine cornstarch and rice wine and stir into the soup.

4. Cook 2-3 minutes to allow cornstarch thicken and clear.

5. Sprinkle with toasted almonds, season and serve.

TIME: Preparation takes 15 minutes, microwave cooking takes 5-8 minutes.

Szechuan Beef

This simple recipe brings out the flavor of the beef.

SERVES 4

1lb rump steak, shredded
2 tbsps oil
½ dried chili pepper, crushed
4 tbsps soy sauce
½ cup stock
2 tbsps cornstarch
3 sticks celery, shredded
1 sweet red pepper, shredded

1. Heat a browning dish for 5 minutes on HIGH.

2. Combine meat and oil and add to the dish. Cook 2 minutes on HIGH in 2 or 3 batches. Re-heat browning dish 2 minutes after each batch.

3. Add the crushed chili pepper.

4. Mix the soy sauce and stock and gradually stir into the cornstarch. Pour over the steak and cook 2-3 minutes.

5. Add the celery and red pepper and mix together with the meat and sauce.

6. Cook a further 1 minute on HIGH until the sauce has thickened but the vegetables are still crisp.

TIME: Preparation takes 20 minutes, microwave cooking takes 6-18 minutes.

COOK'S TIP: Do not substitute a cheaper cut of meat or the final result will be Tough Beef!

SINGAPORE CHICKEN

*Chicken, pineapple and mandarin
form the basis of this colorful dish.*

SERVES 4

2 tbsps oil
2 tsps curry powder
1lb chicken, skinned, boned and cut
   into bite-sized pieces
1 large onion, cut in large pieces
1 tbsp cornstarch
8oz can pineapple chunks, juice
   reserved
10oz can mandarin orange segments,
   juice reserved
1 cup bean sprouts
Dash soy sauce
Salt and pepper

1. Heat the oil in a large casserole dish for 30 seconds on HIGH.

2. Add the curry powder, and cook 30 seconds on HIGH.

3. Add the chicken, cover the dish and cook 5 minutes on HIGH.

4. Add the onion, mix the cornstarch with the reserved pineapple and orange juice and add to the chicken. Cover and cook 5 minutes on HIGH, stirring occasionally after 1 minute.

5. When the sauce thickens, add the pineapple, orange segments and bean sprouts.

6. Leave to stand 2 minutes before serving. Serve with fried or plain boiled rice.

TIME: Preparation takes 20 minutes, microwave cooking takes 11 minutes
plus 2 minutes standing time.

COOK'S TIP: Do not buy the bean sprouts too far in advance as they deteriorate rapidly.

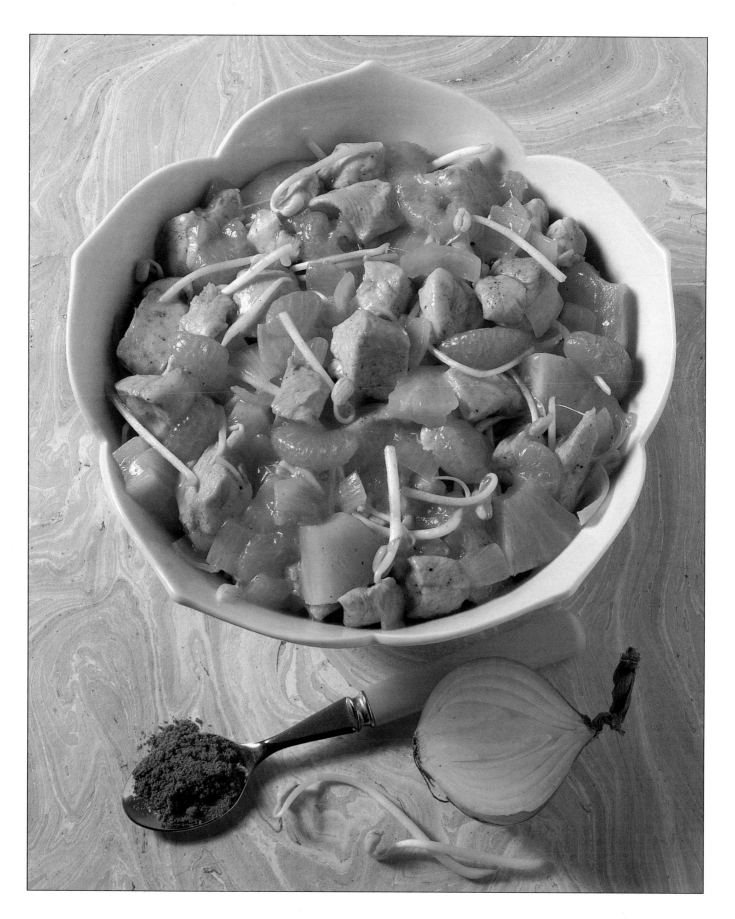

CHICKEN WITH SNOW PEAS

Snow peas bring a flavor all their own to any recipe.

SERVES 4

2 tbsps oil
1lb chicken breasts, skinned, boned and
   cut into thin slivers
2 tsps cornstarch
3 tbsps rice wine
3 tbsps light soy sauce
2 tbsps oyster sauce
4 tbsps chicken stock
Dash sesame oil
Salt and pepper
4oz snow peas

1. Heat the oil 30 seconds on HIGH in a
large casserole dish.

2. Mix the remaining ingredients except
the snow peas, and pour over the
chicken.

3. Cover and cook 7-9 minutes on HIGH,
stirring halfway through cooking time.

4. Add the snow peas, re-cover the dish
and cook 30 seconds on HIGH.

5. Leave to stand for 2 minutes before
serving. Serve with rice.

TIME: Preparation takes 20 minutes, microwave cooking takes 8½-9½ minutes
plus 2 minutes standing time.

BUYING GUIDE: Oyster sauce is a common ingredient in Chinese cooking and
is widely available in supermarkets.

Duck with Pineapple

A great combination that always goes down well.

SERVES 4

Sauce
8oz can crushed pineapple, or
   1 fresh pineapple, peeled and cored
1½ tsps cornstarch dissolved in
   1 tbsp water
1 tbsp light soy sauce
1½ tsps sugar
1 tbsp white wine
1 piece ginger root, grated
Pinch salt

5lb duckling
2 tbsps oil
2 tbsps soy sauce

Garnish
4 chives, shredded

1. If using fresh pineapple, work in a food processor until finely chopped. Add remaining sauce ingredients and mix well in a small, deep bowl. Cook 4 minutes on HIGH until the sauce thickens and clears.

2. Skin the duck and remove the leg and breast meat. Cut into thin slivers.

3. Heat a browning dish 5 minutes on HIGH. Toss the oil and duck together, and add to the browning dish. Cook, uncovered, 4 minutes on HIGH.

4. Add the soy sauce, cover the dish and reduce the setting to MEDIUM. Cook a further 3 minutes or until duck is tender.

5. Remove duck to a serving dish and keep warm. Coat with the pineapple sauce and sprinkle on the chives. Serve with rice.

TIME: Preparation takes 20 minutes, microwave cooking takes 9-10 minutes.

SWEET-SOUR CABBAGE

The perfect refreshing side dish.

SERVES 4

1 medium head white cabbage,
   about 2lbs
1 small red chili pepper (use less if
   desired)
½ cup light brown sugar
⅓ cup rice wine vinegar
2 tbsps light soy sauce
Salt
3 tbsps oil

1. Cut the cabbage into ½-inch slices,
discarding the core. Cut the chili pepper
into thin, short strips, discarding the seeds.

2. Mix all the ingredients together except
the oil.

3. Pour the oil into a large bowl and heat
for 2 minutes on HIGH.

4. Add the cabbage and the liquid and
cover the bowl with pierced plastic wrap.
Cook on HIGH for 9-11 minutes.

5. Allow to cool in the bowl, stirring
frequently. When cold, refrigerate.

TIME: Preparation takes 20 minutes, microwave cooking takes 11-13 minutes.

COOK'S TIP: Vary the amount of sugar and chili pepper according to your own taste.

Ten Varieties of Beauty

*The name of this recipe refers to the variety
of vegetables in the recipe.*

SERVES 4-6

4 tbsps oil
3 sticks celery, diagonally sliced
2 carrots, peeled and cut into ribbons with
 a vegetable peeler
3oz snow peas
1 red pepper, thickly sliced
8 ears of baby corn
4 green onions, diagonally sliced
1 cup bean sprouts
10 water chestnuts, sliced
½ small can sliced bamboo shoots
10 Chinese dried mushrooms, soaked in
 hot water, stalks removed
1¼ cups chicken stock
2 tbsps cornstarch
3 tbsps light soy sauce
Sesame oil

1. Heat a browning dish for 5 minutes on
HIGH. Pour in the oil and add the celery
and carrots. Cook for 1 minute on HIGH.

2. Remove from the dish and add the
snow peas, red pepper and corn. Cook for
1 minute on HIGH and place with the
celery and carrots.

3. Add the onions, bean sprouts, water
chestnuts and bamboo shoots to the dish.
Cook for 1 minute on HIGH, adding the
mushrooms after 30 seconds.

4. Place with the rest of vegetables.

5. Combine the rest of the ingredients in a
glass measure. Cook 2-3 minutes on HIGH
until thickened. Taste and add salt if
necessary. Pour over the vegetables and
stir carefully.

6. Reheat for 1-2 minutes on HIGH before
serving.

TIME: Preparation takes 20 minutes, microwave cooking takes 6-8 minutes.

271

BEANS WITH BAMBOO SHOOTS

An unusual combination which is wonderfully tasty.

SERVES 4

6 pieces Chinese black fungi (tree or wood ears), soaked 30 minutes
8oz green beans, cut into 2 inch diagonal pieces
2 whole pieces canned bamboo shoots, cut into thin triangular pieces
2 tbsps oil
2 tbsps soy sauce
2 tsps cornstarch
4 tbsps light stock and wine mixed
Dash sesame oil
Salt and pepper

1. Heat a browning dish for 5 minutes on HIGH. Pour in the oil and add the beans and bamboo shoots. Cook, uncovered, for 2 minutes on HIGH.
2. Add the tree ears, cover the dish and leave to stand while preparing the sauce.
3. Mix the remaining ingredients except the sesame oil in a glass measure. Cook for 2 minutes on HIGH, stirring once until thickened.
4. Combine with the vegetables and stir in the sesame oil to serve.

TIME: Preparation takes 30 minutes, microwave cooking takes 4 minutes.

SPICY CUCUMBERS

This refreshing side dish is perfect served with a spicy main course.

SERVES 4

1 large cucumber
Salt
3 tbsps light soy sauce
Pinch five-spice powder
¼ tsp crushed red pepper
2 tsps sesame oil
1 tbsp rice vinegar
3 tbsps Chinese parsley leaves (cilantro leaves)

1. Peel thin strips off the cucumber with a canelle knife for a white and green striped effect. Cut in half lengthwise, or in quarters if the cucumber is thick. Cut the lengths into 2-inch pieces. Sprinkle with salt and leave to stand 30 minutes.

2. Wash and dry well. Combine the cucumber with all the remaining ingredients, except the parsley, in a deep bowl. Partially cover and cook for 2 minutes on HIGH.

3. Add the parsley and leave in the bowl to cool. When cold, refrigerate. Serve on the same day.

TIME: Preparation takes 30 minutes, microwave cooking takes 2 minutes.

ALMOND COOKIES

In China these biscuits are often eaten as a between-meal snack. In Western-style cuisine, they make a good accompaniment to fruit or sherbet.

MAKES 30 COOKIES

½ cup butter or margarine
4 tbsps superfine sugar
2 tbsps light brown sugar
1 egg, beaten
Almond extract
1 cup all-purpose flour
1 tsp baking powder
Pinch salt
1oz ground almonds, blanched or
    unblanched
2 tbsps water
30 whole blanched almonds

1. Cream the butter or margarine together with the two sugars until light and fluffy.

2. Divide the beaten egg in half and add half to the sugar mixture with a few drops of the almond essence and beat until smooth. Reserve the remaining egg for later use. Sift the flour, baking powder and salt into the egg mixture and add the ground almonds. Stir well by hand.

3. Shape the mixture into small balls and place well apart on a lightly greased cookie sheet. Flatten slightly and press an almond on to the top of each one.

4. Mix the reserved egg with the water and brush each cookie before baking.

5. Place in a preheated 350°F oven and bake for 12-15 minutes. Cookies will be a pale golden color when done.

TIME: Preparation takes about 10 minutes. If the dough becomes too soft, refrigerate for 10 minutes before shaping. Cooking takes about 12-15 minutes per batch.

COOK'S TIP: Roll the mixture on a floured surface with floured hands to prevent sticking.

WATCHPOINT: Do not over beat once the almonds are added. They will begin to oil and the mixture will become too soft and sticky to shape.

SERVING IDEA: Serve with fruit, ice cream or sherbet.

FREEZING: Cookies may be frozen baked or unbaked. Defrost uncooked dough completely at room temperature before baking. Baked cookies may be re-crisped by heating in the oven for about 2 minutes and then allowed to cool before serving.

MELON SALAD

*A refreshing fruit salad, which is especially tasty
served after a heavy meal of many courses.*

SERVES 4

1 large cantaloupe melon
1 mango
4 canned litchis
4 large or 8 small strawberries
Litchi syrup from the can

1. Peel and seed the melon and cut into thin slices.

2. Peel and pit the mango and cut into thin slices.

3. Using a melon baller, cut as many balls as possible out the strawberries.

4. Arrange the melon slices evenly on 4 small plates.

5. Spread a layer of mango over the melon. Place a litchi in the center of each plate and arrange a few strawberry balls around the edges.

6. Divide the litchi syrup evenly between the plates of fruit and chill them in the refrigerator before serving.

TIME: Preparation takes about 30 minutes.

VARIATION: Use a honeydew melon instead of the cantaloupe variety.

COOK'S TIP: This dessert is best served well chilled from the refrigerator, so prepare it several hours in advance of serving.

Maltose

A molasses-like substance which is made by fermenting barley or a similar grain. It can be substituted in recipes by honey, corn syrup or treacle.

Monosodium Glutamate

This is a white crytalline substance used extensively in Chinese cooking for tenderizing meat and enhancing the flavor of dishes. It should be used sparingly as too much will spoil the dish. It can be totally omitted without unduly altering the taste of a dish.

Dried Mushrooms

Tree Fungus found in the East on oak logs and Shii trees. They are sold dried and have to be reconstituted by soaking in hot water. They are expensive, but only a few are needed to impart their distinctive woody flavor to a dish.

Noodles

There are many different kinds of noodles. Some are made from wheat flour, some from rice flour and some from bean flour. Egg noodles can be either thin or thick. The thin noodles are sold in "cakes" whereas the thick noodles are spaghetti like and are often called Shanghai noodles. Bean Thread noodles are thin, white noodles which go transparent when cooked. They are mostly used in soups and stews and should be soaked before use. Rice Stick noodles are very thin noodles.

Oyster Sauce

This is a special sauce produced from soy sauce and oysters which have been fermented together. It is now widely available in supermarkets.

Rice

There are many different varieties of rice. Long grained rice is the variety usually used for making simple rice dishes. Basmati is the finest and most expensive long-grain rice. Glutinous rice is also common in Chinese cooking. It is a medium-grain rice used for making puddings and savoury dishes.

Sesame Oil

An aromatic oil produced from sesame seeds. This has a special flavor and is used as a seasoning and is a vital ingredient in some sauces. It is available from most good supermarkets.

Soy Sauce

There are two different types; one is

dark and the other is light. Both are used for flavoring nearly all Chinese foods. The dark soy sauce is stronger in flavor and thicker, whilst the light soy sauce is a weaker infusion.

Star Anise

This is an eight-pointed clove with a strong anise smell and flavor. It can be purchased as a powder or whole.

Szechuan Pickle

This salty pickle is made from cabbage, chilies and mustard and has a strong flavor. It is sold in jars and cans and is available from Chinese supermarkets.

Water Chestnuts

These are the bulb-like stems of the bulrush. They are slightly sweet and have a crisp texture.

Index